Lecture Notes in Control and Information Sciences

Edited by A. V. Balakrishnan and M. Thoma

Lecture Notes in Control and Information Sciences

Edited by A.V. Balakrishnan and M. Thoma

4

M. A. Crane · A. J. Lemoine

An Introduction
to the Regenerative Method
for Simulation Analysis

Springer-Verlag
Berlin Heidelberg GmbH 1977

Series Editors
A. V. Balakrishnan · M. Thoma

Advisory Board
A. G. J. MacFarlane · H. Kwakernaak · Ya. Z. Tsypkin

Authors
Dr. M. A. Crane
Dr. A. J. Lemoine

Control Analysis Corporation
800 Welch Road
Palo Alto, California 94304, USA

With 4 Figures

ISBN 978-3-540-08408-2   ISBN 978-3-540-37175-5 (eBook)
DOI 10.1007/978-3-540-37175-5

PREFACE

Many real-world problems involve systems of a random nature, i.e., stochastic systems. Examples of such systems are communications networks, queues
and queueing networks, inspection, maintenance and repair operations, and inventory systems. Many of these systems are quite complicated, and the most practical approach to their study is through simulation.

In simulating systems of a random nature, it is important that a convincing statistical analysis be applied to the output of the simulation. In particular, estimation techniques are needed which permit the simulator to make
valid statistical inferences about the model based on simulation output. Such
techniques are also essential so that the simulator may address the important
tradeoffs between simulation run length and the level of precision in the estimates.

Until recently, however, the statistical methodology available to simulators for analyzing the output of simulations of stochastic systems has been
quite limited. Under these circumstances, simulators often find it difficult
to perform adequate statistical analyses; so difficult, in fact, that such
important factors as confidence levels and precision of estimates are sometimes
virtually ignored.

A new technique of analysis called the regenerative method has recently
been developed to deal with these problems. The method can produce valid and
substantive statistical results for a very large and important set of simulations of systems with random elements. In fact, the regenerative method has
already been successfully applied to a broad variety of practical problems.
Moreover, it provides a simple solution to the difficult "tactical" problems
of how to start the simulation, when to begin collecting data, how long to run
the simulation, and how to deal with highly correlated output.

Given this important development, the goal of this "tutorial" is to present the basic ideas and results of the regenerative method in a manner which may be easily understood by all potential users. The background required for following the presentation is not extensive: a basic introduction to probability and statistics (including the central limit theorem and the notion of a confidence interval) and some acquaintance with the notion of modeling for problem solving. A concerted attempt has been made to keep the narrative informal but precise, without inundating the reader in theorems, propositions, and formalities. Extensive use is made of examples to motivate and to illustrate fundamental ideas and results. Markov chains are used in certain examples, but readers unfamiliar with the concept of a Markov chain can safely ignore those places in the narrative where they appear without missing basic ideas or results.

ACKNOWLEDGEMENT

It is a pleasure to express our gratitude to David Snyder and James Sylvester, both of Control Analysis Corporation. They reviewed an earlier draft of this tutorial and made a number of excellent suggestions which have been incorporated into the current version. James Sylvester provided programming assistance for the simulation runs reported in Section 3 and Section 4. The superb technical typing of this tutorial is the work of Evelyn Morris.

This work was supported by the Office of Naval Research (ONR) under contract N00014-72-C-0086 (NR-047-106). We are grateful to Dr. Thomas C. Varley of ONR for his advice and encouragement.

TABLE OF CONTENTS

TABLE OF CONTENTS (Cont'd)

LIST OF TABLES AND FIGURES

1.0 INTRODUCTION

Many important problems arising in operations research and systems analysis are too complex to be resolved by formulating and solving mathematical models. Simulation often provides the only practical approach to such problems. This is certainly the case for many stochastic systems, i.e., systems with random elements. Such systems include a broad variety of queues and queueing networks, inventory systems, inspection, maintenance, and repair operations, and numerous other situations. And it is indeed the simulation of stochastic systems that will concern us here.

The simulation of a stochastic system should be viewed as a statistical experiment. We first construct a model of the system which captures the essence of the problem by revealing its underlying structure and providing insight into the cause-and-effect relationships within the system. With the aid of a computer we then perform sampling experiments on the model and analyze the output data to make inferences about the behavior of the system. Our simulation experiments, therefore, are virtually the same as ordinary statistical experiments, and so must be based on sound statistical procedures in order to produce meaningful results. In particular, estimation techniques are needed, e.g., methods of obtaining confidence intervals, which permit the simulator to make valid statistical inferences about the model based on simulation output. Such techniques are also essential so that the simulator may address the important tradeoffs between simulation run length and the level of precision in the estimates.

However, most stochastic simulations of interest are far more complex than the sort of experiments which are analyzed by classical methods of statistics. Thus, the statistical methodology available to simulators for analyzing the output of such simulations has been very meager. Under these circumstances, simulators have often found it difficult, if not impossible, to carry out adequate statistical analyses of the output of stochastic simulations.

In the last four years a statistical methodology has been developed for analyzing the output of the class of regenerative simulations, which, as we shall see, form a very large and very interesting class of simulations. The regenerative approach is motivated by the fact that many stochastic systems have the property of "starting afresh probabilistically" from time to time. This enables the simulator to observe independent and identically distributed blocks of data in the course of the simulation, thereby facilitating statistical analysis. Moreover, the regenerative approach provides a simple solution to the difficult "tactical" problems of how to start the simulation, when to begin collecting data, how long to run the simulation, and how to deal with highly correlated output.

The research efforts which have led to the regenerative approach have been supported by the Office of Naval Research. The study efforts have now reached a certain level of maturity. Many results of practical interest are available, and these are of sufficient scope to justify an informal account of the work done thus far. We provide such an account here, and it is our goal to present the basic results of the regenerative approach in a manner which may be easily understood by all potential users.

The background required for following this presentation is not extensive: a basic introduction to probability and statistics and some acquaintance with the notion of modeling for problem solving. A concerted attempt has been made to keep the narrative informal but precise, without inundating the reader in theorems, propositions, and formalities. Extensive use is made of examples to motivate and to illustrate fundamental ideas and results. It is hoped that readers will indeed find these examples to be helpful.

This tutorial presentation is organized as follows:

Section	Title
1	INTRODUCTION AND SUMMARY
2	BASIC EXAMPLES AND MOTIVATION
3	THE REGENERATIVE METHOD
4	MORE EXAMPLES OF REGENERATIVE PROCESSES
5	THE REGENERATIVE APPROACH AND DISCRETE-EVENT SIMULATIONS
6	APPROXIMATION PROCEDURES
7	ALTERNATIVE RATIO ESTIMATORS
8	SOME OTHER RESULTS
9	BIBLIOGRAPHIC NOTE
	REFERENCES

The current section introduces and summarizes the presentation. The second section presents some basic examples which serve to illustrate the problems and issues that arise in analyzing the output of stochastic simulations. The traditional "tactical" problems of correlation of simulation output and bias toward initial conditions are addressed. The examples of Section 2 also serve to motivate the regenerative approach as a means of resolving these problems and issues.

4

The fundamental ideas of the regenerative method are then spelled out in
Section 3. Procedures are given for making valid statistical inferences
about model parameters based on simulation output. In particular, a method
is given for obtaining a confidence interval for the expected value of an
arbitrary function of the steady-state distribution of the process being
simulated. The method is based on a random blocking technique which enables
the simulator to group the output data into independent and identically distributed blocks. More examples of regenerative processes are given in Section
4 to further the reader's understanding of the approach. In Section 5 we present a simple and unifying frame of reference for all discrete-event regenerative simulations, and it is shown how general discrete-event simulations are
related to the regenerative approach. Approximation procedures which are
useful when the regenerative approach is not directly applicable are indicated
in Section 6. In Section 7 we discuss ratio estimators, as the problem of
ratio estimation arises whenever the regenerative method is used. In Section
8 we discuss some other results which have been developed for the regenerative
method, and all of these results are concerned with important topics of practical interest to simulators. These results include a methodology to compare
the performance of several systems which are being simulated, a methodology
for estimating quantiles of steady-state distributions, a technique for
gauging the sensitivity of statistical inferences relative to changes in the
input parameters for the simulation experiment, discrete-time methods for
continuous-time problems which can produce considerable savings in computing
time as well as increased statistical efficiency, investigations into stopping

rules in simulations of stable stochastic systems, and methods for reducing the variance of estimators of steady-state parameters in regenerative simulations. The final section, Section 9, provides a brief survey of the relevant literature on the regenerative approach for stochastic simulations.

2.0 BASIC EXAMPLES AND MOTIVATION

In this section we present three simple but important examples of
systems which occur frequently in applications: a single-server queue, a
periodic review inventory system, and a repair model for maintaining a
group of on-line operating units. The point of view will be that of a
simulator who is given the task of simulating each system in order to pre-
dict how the system will behave. These examples will dilineate the difficult issues faced by the simulator in carrying out this task in a satisfactory manner, and will also serve to motivate the basic ideas of the
regenerative method as a simple approach for resolving these issues. We
start with the queueing system.

2.1 A Single-Server Queue

The standard single-server queue is depicted in Figure 2.1.
Customers originate from an input source which generates new customers one
at a time. If an arriving customer finds the server free his service

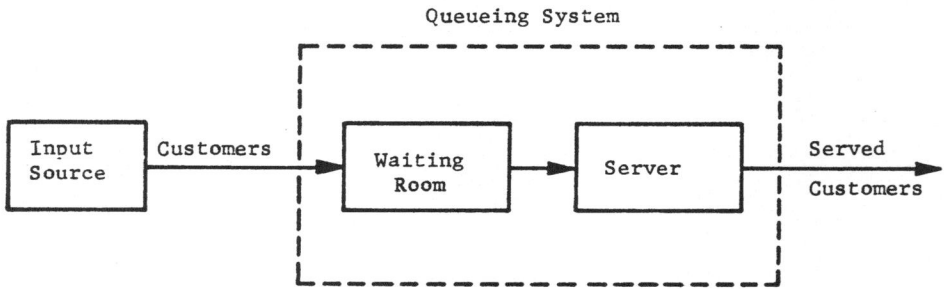

Figure 2.1 - Single-Server Queue

commences immediately and he departs from the system when his service requirements have been satisfied. If the arriving customer finds the server occupied, he enters the waiting room and waits his turn to be served. Customers are transfered from the queue into service on a first-come-first-served basis.

For the particular queueing system under consideration, suppose that the input source generates a new customer every 60 seconds. Further, suppose that the service requirements of successive customers are independent random variables that are uniformly distributed on the range from 10 seconds to 90 seconds. Assume the measure of performance to be used for the system is $E\{W\}$, the mean value of the waiting time (exclusive of service time) experienced by a customer under steady-state conditions. Since no computationally tractable analytical results are available for calculating the exact value of $E\{W\}$ in this particular system, simulation is a natural recourse.

Therefore, the task is one of simulating the system and analyzing the output to provide an estimate for the value of $E\{W\}$. Furthermore, it would be desirable to obtain some measure of the "reliability" of the estimate for $E\{W\}$, e.g., a 90% confidence interval for the true value of $E\{W\}$, so that the simulator can determine whether more lengthy runs are required to obtain acceptable precision in the results.

A reasonable way to proceed would seem to be as follows. Let W_1 denote the waiting time of the first customer in the simulated system, W_2

the waiting time of the second customer, and so on. Then, if the total
duration of the simulation run is for N customers, where N might be
1000, for example, then the sample average

$$\frac{W_1 + W_2 + \cdot \cdot \cdot + W_N}{N} \tag{2.1}$$

is a "consistent estimator" for $E\{W\}$, since it is known that the sample
average converges to the true value of $E\{W\}$ with probability one as
$N \to \infty$. However, the sample average (2.1) will in general be a "biased
estimator" for the true value of $E\{W\}$ due to the initial conditions.
For example, if W_1 is given the value zero, as is usually the case, then
the first few waiting times will tend to be small. Such bias can be elimi-
nated if the simulator can choose a value for W_1 by sampling from the
distribution of W itself. Unfortunately, the simulator does not even
know the mean of W , let alone its distribution, so that this "solution"
is not very practical.

The traditional way of dealing with the difficulty of the initial
bias is to run the simulation model for some time without collecting data
until it is believed that the simulated queueing system has essentially
reached a steady-state condition and then to collect data from that point on.

For example, we might simulate the system for 2000 customers, discard the waiting times of the first 1000 customers, and use the average

$$\frac{W_{1001} + \cdots + W_{2000}}{1000}$$

as an estimate for $E\{W\}$. But, it is by no means clear just how long this "stabilization" period ought to be, so that a great deal of unproductive computer time can be wasted in the process.

There is also another difficulty with using the "seemingly reasonable" estimation procedure which starts with the sample average in (2.1). Based on the output of the simulation experiment, we would like to obtain some measure of the "reliability" of the estimate for $E\{W\}$, indicating the likelihood that similar estimates would result if we were to repeat the simulation. In this spirit, we might wish to construct a 90% confidence interval $\underline{I}$ for the true value of $E\{W\}$, such that in any independent replication of the simulation experiment, the probability would be 0.90 of having the computed interval $\underline{I}$ include the true value for $E\{W\}$. However, in order to construct such confidence intervals using classical statistics, the output data must form a collection of statistically independent and identically distributed samples from some underlying probability distribution. The output data from the queueing simulation is the sequence of waiting times W_1 , W_2 , $\ldots$, W_N . Note, however, that if W_k is large, then the next customer, $k + 1$, will typically have a large waiting time also; and conversely, if W_k is small, then W_{k+1} will tend to be small. Thus, the samples W_k and W_{k+1} are highly correlated, and this is true whether or not the simulation is begun by sampling from the steady-state distribution of W . Thus, since the waiting times W_1 , W_2 , . . . , W_N are not independent, classical statistics appears to be of little use in assessing the "reliability" of (2.1) as an estimate for $E\{W\}$.

We see, therefore, that the bias due to the initial conditions and the highly correlated output data pose serious obstacles to using the proposed estimation procedure based on the sample average of (2.1). Since the sample average is such a simple and natural way to estimate $E\{W\}$, these "tactical difficulties" raise doubts about whether or not the simulation experiment for the queueing system will lead to meaningful results. We must ask, therefore, if there might be a simple way to overcome these obstacles which does not require the use of sophisticated or cumbersome methods of analysis. Fortunately, the answer to this question is yes, and we can accomplish this by proceeding in a very straightforward manner.

Suppose we begin the simulation by setting $W_1 = 0$, that we then run the simulation for a short while, and that the customer waiting times observed are as in Figure 2.2. We see that customers 1,3,9,10,13 and 20 are the lucky ones who find the server idle when they arrive and consequently experience no waiting in the queue, while customers 2,4,5,6,7,8,11,12,14,15,16,17,18 and 19 are obliged to wait before being served. Moreover, the server is constantly busy from the time of arrival of customer 1 to the time of departure of customer 2, then constantly idle until customer 3 appears, busy while serving customers 3,4, 5,6,7 and 8, idle from the time customer 8 leaves until customer 9 arrives, then

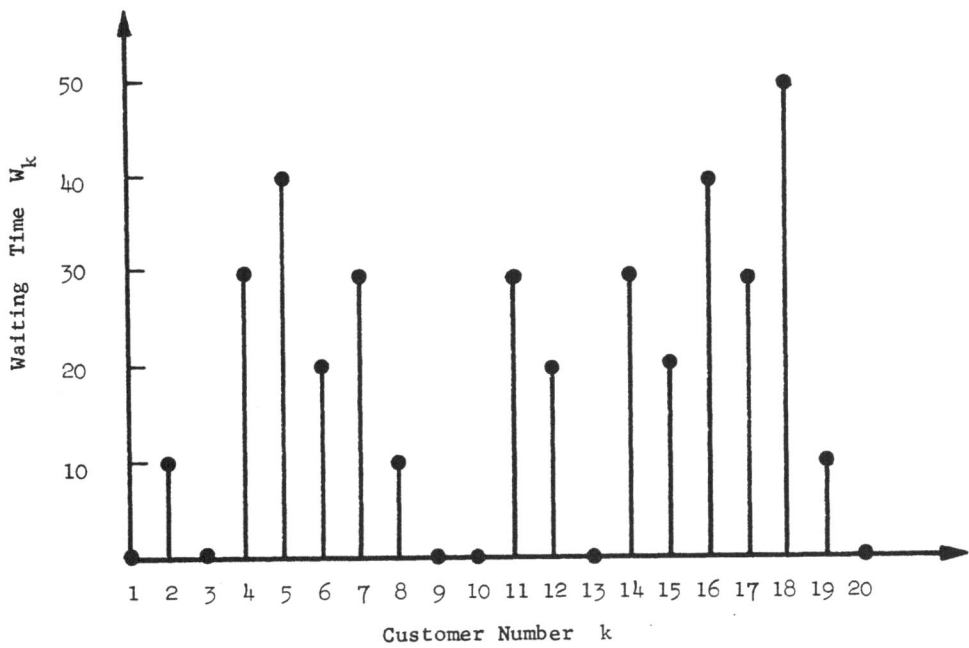

Figure 2.2 - Sample output of queueing simulation

busy until customer 9 departs, and so on. Now had we run the simulation

beyond customer 20 until we had processed 1000 customers, say, then the simu-

lated queue would undoubtedly exhibit the same pattern of the server being

busy, then idle, then busy, then idle, and so on. Suppose we call the opera-

tional span of a "busy period" and its ensuing "idle period" a "cycle." Then,

our short simulation run has 5 complete cycles during which the following

sets of customers are processed by the system: {1,2},{3,4,5,6,7,8},{9},{10,11,12},

{13,14,15,16,17,18,19} . A sixth cycle begins with the arrival of customer 20.

Thus, each new cycle is initiated by a customer who finds the server idle upon

arriving.

Note that the system "begins anew" at the dawn of each cycle as it did when customer 1 arrived. That is, at the time when a cycle commences, the future evolution of the simulated queueing system is always independent of its past behavior and always governed by the same probabilistic structure as when customer 1 arrived to find an idle server. The same is also true of the corresponding "real world" queueing system. The start of each cycle is indistinguishable from the arrival of the very first customer to the queue. It seems natural, therefore, to group the simulation output data into blocks, the first block consisting of the waiting times of customers in the first cycle, the second block consisting of the waiting times of customers in the second cycle, and so on. For the short simulation run illustrated above the blocks are $\{W_1, W_2\}$, $\{W_3, W_4, W_5, W_6, W_7, W_8\}$, $\{W_9\}$, $\{W_{10}, W_{11}, W_{12}\}$, and $\{W_{13}, W_{14}, W_{15}, W_{16}, W_{17}, W_{18}, W_{19}\}$. Thus, since each cycle is initiated under the same conditions, and the system "starts afresh" at the times when cycles commence, the blocks of data from successive cycles are statistically independent, and also possess the same distribution. So, for example, if we set Y_k equal to the sum of the waiting times of customers processed in cycle k, and α_k equal to the number of customers processed in cycle k, the pairs (Y_1, α_1), (Y_2, α_2), (Y_3, α_3), (Y_4, α_4) and (Y_5, α_5) are independent and identically distributed. (Note, however that Y_k and α_k are highly correlated.) From Figure 2.1 we have the following:

$$(Y_1, \alpha_1) = (10, 2)$$
$$(Y_2, \alpha_2) = (130, 6)$$
$$(Y_3, \alpha_3) = (0, 1)$$
$$(Y_4, \alpha_4) = (50, 3)$$
$$(Y_5, \alpha_5) = (180, 7)$$

Hence, the highly correlated data $\{W_1, W_2, \ldots, W_{19}\}$ has been broken up into statistically independent and identically distributed blocks.

Now, at this point the reader might stop and remark that what we have just observed is all very good but what does it do towards solving the difficult problems we face in analyzing the simulation output, i.e., of obtaining a valid estimate for $E\{W\}$. Suppose we resume the simulation run with customer 20 and continue until we have observed n complete cycles of the sort identified above. As before, let Y_k and α_k denote, respectively, the sum of the waiting times of those customers processed in cycle k and the number of customers processed in cycle k, for $k = 1, 2, \ldots, n$. Then, if N is the total number of customers processed over the n cycles, observe that

$$\frac{W_1 + W_2 + \ldots + W_N}{N} = \frac{Y_1 + \ldots + Y_n}{\alpha_1 + \ldots + \alpha_n} \quad . \tag{2.2}$$

The right side of (2.2) can be written as

$$\frac{(Y_1 + \ldots + Y_n)/n}{(\alpha_1 + \ldots + \alpha_n)/n} \quad . \tag{2.3}$$

Since each of $\{Y_1, \ldots, Y_n\}$ and $\{\alpha_1, \ldots, \alpha_n\}$ is a collection of independent and identically distributed random variables, we know by the law of large numbers that the numerator in (2.3) converges to the value of $E\{Y_1\}$ as $n \to \infty$ and the denominator converges to the value of $E\{\alpha_1\}$ as $n \to \infty$, both with probability one. Note that $N \geq n$, and that $N \to \infty$ as $n \to \infty$. Moreover, we have already observed that the left side of (2.2) converges to the value of $E\{W\}$ as $N \to \infty$, with probability one. Hence, we have proven that

$$E\{W\} = E\{Y_1\}/E\{\alpha_1\} \quad . \tag{2.4}$$

Therefore, the problem of estimating $E\{W\}$ is the same as estimating the ratio $E\{Y_1\}/E\{\alpha_1\}$. And, since this ratio can be estimated from the independent and identically distributed pairs $(Y_1 , \alpha_1), \ldots , (Y_n , \alpha_n)$, classical statistics can be used to make inferences about the true value of $E\{W\}$ based on the simulation output. In particular, we can construct a confidence interval for $E\{Y_1\}/E\{\alpha_1\}$, and a procedure for doing so will be given in Section 3.

Thus, we have arrived at a simple solution of what to do about the highly correlated output data from the simulated queueing system. Moreover, by taking $W_1 = 0$ we begin the simulation by initiating a cycle, and thus no stabilization period whatever is required and every piece of output data generated by the simulation is useful in obtaining a statistically sound estimate of $E\{W\}$.

So, we see that our short simulation run has provided us with insight on how to resolve the hard "tactical" problems we faced at the outset of the proposed simulation experiment; namely, the problem of how to begin the simulation, the problem of when to start collecting data, and the problem of highly correlated output.

At this point it would be well to pause and take stock of what has been done. We began with the goal of estimating the expected steady-state waiting time in a single-server queue by simulating the system and analyzing the output. Before we could even start the simulation experiment, however, we found ourselves facing difficult tactical issues which had to be resolved in order for us to carry out a meaningful statistical analysis of the simulation output. Not to be dissuaded, we then observed that the behavior of the simulated system was characterized by a succession of cycles, that the system regenerated itself probabilistically at the dawn of each cycle, and that if the simulation output were grouped into blocks, with each block consisting of output from a particular cycle, then the blocks were statistically independent, identically distributed, and, in view of (2.4), carried valuable information about the steady-state parameter to be estimated. Thus, the difficult tactical issues were resolved, and we could proceed with our simulation experiment.

Now, if this notion of a stochastic simulation "regenerating itself" probabilistically can be applied to simulations other than queueing, then we have discovered an approach which could be very helpful in analyzing the output of a large class of stochastic simulations. So, we will now see if this idea of regeneration goes further by looking at two other stochastic systems which occur frequently in applications, a periodic review inventory model and a model of repair operations for a group of on-line operating units.

2.2   An Inventory System

Consider now a model of a supply depot stocking a variety of items.
Certain of these items are more critical than others, and if a request comes
in for one of these important items and none is in stock then a high penalty
is incurred in terms of reduced operational efficiency or readiness by the
user requesting the item. Interest here will center on one particular type
of critical item.

Suppose that the inventory level of the item in question is checked at
the beginning of consecutive time intervals of equal length called "periods."
Suppose also that there are 9 users of the item and each user will need a
unit in a typical period with probability 1/3. Thus, the total demand for
the item in a typical period has a binomial distribution with parameters 9
and 1/3. Demands in successive periods are independent. Assume that since
the item is critical it can be delivered almost instantaneously from the
supplier, so that the delivery time is negligible compared to the length of
a period. Penalties for shortages are assessed at $1,000 per shortage per
period. However, the item requires substantial storage capacity, and so
there is a holding cost of $250 per item carried per period. Thus, the
manager of the supply depot seeks an appropriate level of the item to stock
so as to strike some balance between high penalties for shortages and loss of
storage capacity for other critical items due to overstocking(i.e., holding costs).

Suppose the following ordering policy is suggested to the inventory
manager. When there are less than 3 units of the item on hand at the beginning
of a period, place an order which raises the inventory level to 7 units; otherwise

do not order. In order to evaluate this policy, the manager is interested in knowing its implication in terms of the average cost per period under steady-state conditions. That is, if the suggested ordering policy is followed and X is the inventory level on hand immediately after the ordering decision under conditions of steady-state, and D is the demand in the period, then the manager seeks to know the value of

$$1{,}000 \cdot E\{(D - X)^+\} + 250 \cdot E\{(X - D)^+\} \ ,$$

where $u^+ = \max(u, 0)$ for any real number u . Since $(u - v)^+ = u - \min(u, v)$, the above expression can be rewritten as

$$1{,}000 \cdot E\{D\} + 250 \cdot E\{X\} - 1{,}250 \cdot E\{\min(X, D)\} \ .$$

But $E\{D\} = 3$, and so the manager's problem is one of finding the values of $E\{X\}$ and $E\{\min(X, D)\}$ when the suggested ordering policy is used. Let us address the problem of estimating these quantities through simulation.

Now, the output of the simulated inventory system will be a sequence of pairs (X_1, D_1) , (X_2, D_2) , . . . , (X_N, D_N) , where X_k is the inventory level after the ordering decision and (instantaneous) delivery, if any, in period k , and D_k is the demand for the item in period k . The sample averages

$$\frac{X_1 + \ldots + X_N}{N} \qquad\qquad (2.5)$$

18

and

$$\frac{\min(X_1, D_1) + \ldots + \min(X_N, D_N)}{N} \qquad (2.6)$$

converge to $E\{X\}$ and $E\{\min(X,D)\}$, respectively, as $N \to \infty$ with probability one. But, unless X_1 is obtained by sampling from the steady-state
distribution of X , which is unknown to the simulator, then the sample
average in (2.5) will be a biased estimate of $E\{X\}$ and the sample average
in (2.6) will be a biased estimate of $E\{\min(X,D)\}$. Moreover, for any k ,
the inventory levels X_k and X_{k+1} are highly correlated, since
$X_{k+1} = X_k - D_k$ if $X_k - D_k \geq 3$. Thus, the same basic problems we observed
in the queueing simulation also confront the simulator of the inventory system.
Due to the initial bias of the estimators and the correlation of the observations, it is not possible to apply classical statistics to estimate the steady-
state values of interest.

Now, from a statistical standpoint, the crucial factor in each period
is the inventory level immediately after the decision to order or not to order
has been made. This is so because the ensuing demand in the period is independent of the inventory level, and the demands are independent from one period
to the next and have a common (in this case, binomial) distribution. Moreover,
this post-ordering-decision inventory level is somewhere in the range from 3
to 7 when the decision is not to order and is exactly 7 when the decision is
to order. Thus, the state of the simulated inventory system is exactly the
same at the beginning of each period in which the inventory level after the

ordering decision is precisely 7, and whenever this is the case the system "starts afresh" or "regenerates itself" probabilistically. That is, each time that $X_n = 7$ the ensuing simulation is independent of past behavior and has the same probabilistic behavior as after any other return to this state.[1] Moreover, the same is true of the corresponding "real-world" inventory system.

So, if we repeat in essence what was done for the queueing simulation, then we should have a simple solution for the difficult problems facing the simulator of the inventory system.

Specifically, suppose we set $X_1 = 7$ and run the simulation until a post-ordering-decision inventory level of 7 is once again observed; say this happens at period β_2, where we have set $\beta_1 = 1$. Let the first "cycle" consist of periods $1, \ldots, \beta_2 - 1$ and the first block consist of the pairs (X_k, D_k) for the periods in this first cycle. We then resume the simulation with period β_2 and continue until period β_3, where β_3 is the first period after β_2 in which the post-ordering-decision inventory level is again 7. Let the second cycle consist of periods $\beta_2, \ldots \beta_3 - 1$ and the second block the pairs (X_k, D_k) for the periods in the second cycle. We then resume the simulation with period β_3 and continue until some large number n of such cycles has been observed, and we continue grouping the output pairs into blocks with block j consisting of the data pairs for the periods in cycle j.

---

[1]In this model it turns out that any of the states 3, 4, 5, 6 can also serve as a regeneration state, and we will discuss consequences of having more than one possible regeneration state in Section 3.5.

Since the simulated inventory system starts afresh probabilistically with the first period in each cycle, the successive blocks are statistically independent and identically distributed. Thus, for example, if we let α_j denote the number of periods in the jth cycle, Y_j denote the sum of the observations X_k over the jth block, and Z_j the sum of the observations $\min(X_k, D_k)$ over the jth block, then the triples $(Y_1, Z_1, \alpha_1), \ldots,$ (Y_n, Z_n, α_n) are independent and identically distributed

Suppose that the simulation run of n cycles consists exactly of the N time periods. We can then write

$$\frac{X_1 + \ldots X_N}{N} = \frac{(Y_1 + \ldots + Y_n)/n}{(\alpha_1 + \ldots + \alpha_n)/n} \tag{2.7}$$

and

$$\frac{\min(X_1, D_1) + \ldots + \min(X_N, D_N)}{N} = \frac{(Z_1 + \ldots + Z_n)/n}{(\alpha_1 + \ldots + \alpha_n)/n}. \tag{2.8}$$

By the law of large numbers, the ratio on the right side of (2.7) converges to $E\{Y_1\}/E\{\alpha_1\}$ as $n \to \infty$, and the ratio on the right side of (2.8) converges to $E\{Z_1\}/E\{\alpha_1\}$ as $n \to \infty$, both with probability one. Moreover, $N \geq n$, and we already know that left side of (2.7) converges to $E\{X\}$ and the left side of (2.8) to $E\{\min(X, D)\}$ as $N \to \infty$, both with probability one. Thus we have proven that

$$E\{X\} = E\{Y_1\}/E\{\alpha_1\} \tag{2.9}$$

and

$$E\{\min(X,D)\} = E\{Z_1\}/E\{\alpha_1\} \; . \tag{2.10}$$

Therefore, the simulator's task of providing the supply depot manager with meaningful estimates for $E\{X\}$ and $E\{\min(X,D)\}$ can be accomplished by using the independent and identically distributed samples (Y_1, Z_1, α_1), . . . , (Y_n, Z_n, α_n) to obtain point estimates and confidence intervals for the ratios on the right side of (2.9) and of (2.10). The simulator's problem of how to start the simulation and when to collect data is also solved by putting $X_1 = 7$ and grouping the data into blocks determined by the successive cycles. In this way, it is not necessary to disregard any of the initial simulation output.

Thus, we have found that the notion of "regeneration times" provides a framework for a meaningful statistical analysis of the inventory simulation. Now, while this example and the previous queueing example have illustrated the regenerative concept for simulations in which the periods between state transition are of fixed-length, we next consider an application when the transition periods are of variable length.

2.3   A Repairman Model

The model of interest here is depicted in Figure 2.3. Suppose there are 10 identical operating units which are subject to failures. Backing up these 10 operating units are 5 spare units which can be used to replace any of the operating units that fail. At most 10 units can be operating at a given time. A failed unit is sent to a repair facility which operates like a queue with 4 servers, that is, failed units are repaired by one of 4 repairmen on a first-come-first-served basis.

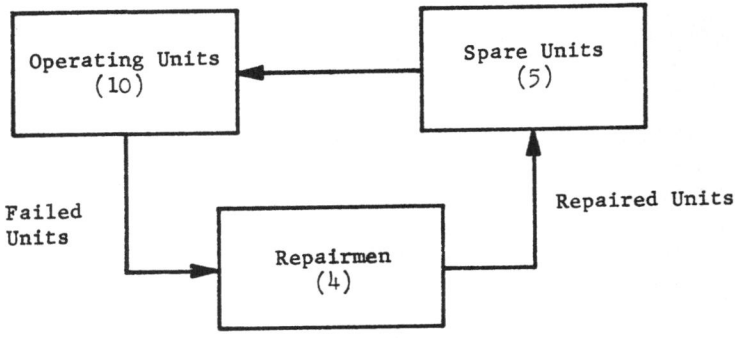

Figure 2.3 - A Repairman Model

Assume that if a unit in "like-new" condition is placed into operation it functions for a random time L until it fails, where the variable L has an exponential distribution with mean 5. The failed unit is sent to the repair facility where it is subsequently restored to "like-new" condition and the time required for a repairman to restore the failed unit is a random variable M which has an exponential distribution with mean 2. After being restored, the unit is returned to the spare pool. Assume that the successive times to failure and the repair times for all units are independent, with all times to failure distributed as L and all repair times distributed as M .

Now, if Y is the number of units in operation under steady-state conditions, then two obvious measures of system performance are $E\{Y\}$ and $P\{Y = 10\}$.

Note, however, that if X is the number of units at the repair facility under steady-state conditions, then

$$Y = 10 - (X - 5)^+ .$$

Thus, the two measures of performance involving Y are equivalent to

$$E\{(X - 5)^+\} \tag{2.12}$$

and.

$$P\{X > 5\} . \tag{2.13}$$

The problem, then, is to estimate the quantities in (2.12) and (2.13) through the use of simulation.

Suppose we simulate the system for T units of time and have as output the values of X(t) for $0 \leq t \leq T$, where X(t) is the number of units at the repair facility at time t . Let f and g be real functions where $f(x) = (x - 5)^+$, $g(x) = 0$ for $x \leq 5$ and $g(x) = 1$ for $x > 5$. Then, a consistent estimator for $E\{(X - 5)^+\}$ is

$$\frac{1}{T} \int_0^T f\big(X(t)\big)\, dt \tag{2.14}$$

and a consistent estimator for $P\{X > 5\}$ is

$$\frac{1}{T} \int_0^T g\bigl(X(t)\bigr) \, dt \qquad\qquad (2.15)$$

since the quantities in (2.14) and (2.15) converge to the values of $E\{(X - 5)^+\}$ and $P\{X > 5\}$, respectively, as $T \to \infty$, both with probability one. This may be seen intuitively by noting that (2.14) gives the time-weighted average of $[X(t) - 5]^+$ and (2.15) gives the fraction of time that $X(t)$ is greater than 5 . However, unless the value of $X(0)$ is sampled from the steady-state distribution of X , both these estimators are biased due to the initial conditions. Moreover, if $s < t$ and s is close to t , then it is obvious that $X(s)$ and $X(t)$ are highly correlated, since the number of units in repair does not change quickly. Thus, we must confront the same basic problems that were present in the queueing and inventory simulations. The bias of the "natural" estimators and the correlation of the observations prevent the use of standard statistical techniques to analyze the simulation output. We shall see, however, that once again the regenerative approach can resolve these difficulties.

We first recall the "lack of memory" property of exponential random variables. As applied to the failure times for the operating units, this property tells us that the time to failure for a unit has the same (exponential) distribution regardless of how long the unit has been operating. In other words, an operating unit is always in a "like-new" condition until it fails; it is no more likely to fail soon if it has been operating for a long time.

Now suppose we begin the simulation assuming we have a "like-new system," that is, 10 units are placed into operation at time 0 and there are 5 new units in the spare pool. Define R_k as the kth time that this "like-new" state is entered, where we set $R_1 \equiv 0$. That is, the R_k's are defined by the times that the repair facility becomes empty. Note, at each of these times there are 10 operating units and 5 fully repaired units in the spare pool. Furthermore, because of the "lack of memory" property of the failure times, the operating units behave identically as they behaved when they were new. Thus, at each time R_k, the system appears identical as it did at time $R_1 = 0$, and its future behavior is also independent of its behavior prior to R_k. In other words, the system "starts afresh" probabilistically, or regenerates itself, at each time R_k. The same is of course true of its "real-world" counterpart.

Now, suppose we run the simulation until we have observed $n + 1$ regeneration times

$$0 = R_1 < R_2 < \ldots < R_n < R_{n+1}$$

where n is a large number. Let block k denote the output data $X(t)$ in the kth regeneration "cycle" from time R_k to time R_{k+1}, that is

$$\left\{ X(t) : R_k \le t < R_{k+1} \right\}$$

for $k = 1, 2, \ldots, n$. Then, since the system "starts afresh" at each epoch R_k, the blocks are independent and identically distributed. So, for example, if we put

$$Y_k = \int_{R_k}^{R_{k+1}} f\big(X(t)\big)\, dt \quad,$$

$$Z_k = \int_{R_k}^{R_{k+1}} g\big(X(t)\big)\, dt \quad,$$

and

$$\alpha_k = R_{k+1} - R_k \quad,$$

with f and g as defined earlier, then the data triples (Y_1, Z_1, α_1), ..., (Y_n, Z_n, α_n) are independent and identically distributed. Moreover, if $R_{n+1} = T$, say, then

$$\frac{1}{T} \int_0^T f\big(X(t)\big)\, dt = \frac{(Y_1 + \ldots + Y_n)n}{(\alpha_1 + \ldots + \alpha_n)/n} \tag{2.17}$$

and

$$\frac{1}{T} \int_0^T g\big(X(t)\big)\, dt = \frac{(Z_1 + \ldots + Z_n)/n}{(\alpha_1 + \ldots + \alpha_n)/n} \tag{2.18}$$

By the law of large numbers, the ratio on the right side of (2.17) converges to $E\{Y_1\}/E\{\alpha_1\}$ as $n \to \infty$, and the ratio on the right side of (2.18) converges to $E\{Z_1\}/E\{\alpha_1\}$ as $n \to \infty$, both with probability one. Moreover as $n \to \infty$ we also have $T \to \infty$, and we have already seen that the left side of (2.17) converges to $E\{(X - 5)^+\}$ as $T \to \infty$ and the left side of (2.18)

converges to $P\{X > 5\}$ as $T \to \infty$, both with probability one. Thus, we

have proven that

$$E\{(X - 5)^+\} = E\{Y_1\}/E\{\alpha_1\} \tag{2.19}$$

and

$$P\{X > 5\} = E\{Z_1\}/E\{\alpha_1\} \quad . \tag{2.20}$$

Thus, the task of obtaining meaningful estimates of (2.12) and (2.13)
via simulation can be achieved by working with the independent and identically
distributed output $(Y_1, Z_1, \alpha_1), \ldots, (Y_n, Z_n, \alpha_n)$ to obtain point estimates and confidence intervals for the ratios on the right side of (2.19) and
of (2.20). Moreover, by starting the simulated system in "like-new" condition
and grouping the output data into blocks determined by successive returns to the
"like-new" condition, it is not necessary to discard any of the initial output
data from the simulation.

2.4   Concluding Remarks

In simulating systems of a random nature, it is important that a
convincing statistical analysis be applied to the output of the simulation.
Such a statistical analysis is necessary so that the parameters of interest

may be estimated and that some indication of the "reliability" of the estimates be made, e.g., through use of confidence intervals. It is only through such reliability measures that the simulator can judge whether the desired precision in the estimates has been obtained or whether more lengthy simulation runs are necessary.

For each of the three examples presented in this section, we observed that if a stochastic system is simulated with the goal of estimating some steady-state parameter, then the simulator faces difficult problems of a "tactical" nature in providing a convincing statistical analysis of the simulation output. These difficult problems include how to start the simulation, when to begin collecting data, and what to do about highly correlated output. We then found, however, that these problems could be overcome (at least for the examples) in a very simple way if the stochastic simulation had the property of "regenerating itself" probabilistically from time to time. We now go on from here to set down a simple framework in Section 3 for analyzing the output of any stochastic simulation having a "regenerative" property of the sort we observed in the examples of this section. We will see that this class of simulations is very broad indeed. Moreover, we will give a simple procedure for constructing a confidence interval (from the simulation output) for a wide variety of steady-state parameters of interest in a "regenerative" simulation.

3.0   THE REGENERATIVE METHOD

The examples of Section 2 suggest a unified approach toward analyzing
the output of those simulations of stochastic systems which have the property
of "regeneration" from time to time. That is, if the simulation output is
viewed as a stochastic process, then these "regenerative processes" have the
property of always returning to some "regenerative condition" from which the
future evolution of the process is always independent of its past behavior and
always governed by the same probability law. If the simulation output is then
grouped into blocks according to successive returns to the "regenerative condition"
then these blocks are statistically independent and identically distributed,
and this greatly facilitates statistical analysis of the output by the simulator.

In this section we shall cast all such "regenerative processes" into a
common framework and then give a simple technique for obtaining a confidence
interval, based on the simulation output, for a variety of steady-state system
parameters of practical interest. The method covers any discrete-event simulation that can be modeled as a regenerative process. A discrete-event simulation is one in which the state of the system being simulated only changes
at a discrete, but possibly random, set of time points. Each of the examples
considered in Section 2 is of this type.

This section is organized as follows. We first discuss regenerative
processes with a discrete time parameter, as in the queueing and inventory
examples, and then regenerative processes with a continuous time parameter, as
in the repairman model. After defining regenerative processes, we then give a
technique for obtaining confidence intervals for steady-state parameters of

such processes and apply this technique to sample simulations of the models of
Section 2. We next discuss the "tactical questions" of run length and of
regeneration points, this latter question arising in the case where a simulation
may have two or more choices of regeneration points. We then observe that the
regenerative method may also be used to estimate the long-run average cost per
unit time, for a general cost function associated with a simulation. Finally,
we close the section by discussing the exact nature of the (very mild) conditions which insure that regenerative processes have steady-state distributions.

3.1 Regenerative Processes in Discrete Time

A sequence $\{X_n, n \geq 1\}$ of random vectors in K dimensions is
a regenerative process if there is an increasing sequence $1 \leq \beta_1 < \beta_2 < \ldots$
of random discrete times, called regeneration epochs, such that at each of these
epochs the process starts afresh probabilistically according to the same probabilistic structure governing it at epoch β_1 . That is, between any two con-
secutive regeneration epochs β_j and β_{j+1} , say, the portion $\{X_n, \beta_j \leq n < \beta_{j+1}\}$
of the process is an independent and identically distributed replicate of the por-
tion between any other two consecutive regeneration epochs. However, the portion
of the process between epoch 1 and epoch β_1 , while independent of the rest of
the process, is allowed to have a different distribution. We will refer to the
portion $\{X_n, \beta_j \leq n < \beta_{j+1}\}$ of the process as the jth cycle.

In the queueing example, $X_n = W_n$, and the epochs of regeneration
$\{\beta_j, j \geq 1\}$ are the indices of those customers who find the server idle upon
their arrival. For the inventory example of Section 2, $X_n = (X_n, D_n)$, and the

regeneration epochs are the periods $\{\beta_j, \ j \geq 1\}$ when the post-ordering-decision inventory level is 7.

A typical situation in which the regenerative assumption is satisfied is when β_j represents the time of the jth entrance to some fixed state, say $\underset{\sim}{s}$. Upon hitting $\underset{\sim}{s}$, the simulation can proceed without any knowledge of its past history. Examples of such epochs are the instants when an arriving customer finds all servers idle in a multi-server queueing system and the times when a recurrent irreducible Markov chain hits a fixed state. Not all regenerative behavior, however, is characterized by returns to a fixed state. For the inventory example of Section 2, regeneration occurs at time n if (X_n, D_n) falls in the set $\{(7, j):j = 0, 1, \ldots, 9\}$, that is, whenever X_n is equal to 7 regardless of D_n . A more general example of this sort will be given in Section 4.1. As these and other examples will show, the class of regenerative simulations is very broad indeed.

Let $\alpha_j = \beta_{j+1} - \beta_j$ for $j \geq 1$. Note that the "sojourn times" $\{\alpha_j, \ j \geq 1\}$ between consecutive epochs of regeneration are independent and identically distributed. We will assume henceforth that $E\{\alpha_1\} < \infty$. This is not a restrictive assumption. For example, it holds in almost any queueing system of practical interest, and it certainly holds for the queueing and inventory examples of Section 2, as well as for any positive recurrent irreducible Markov chain.

The regenerative property is an extremely powerful tool for obtaining analytical results for the process $\{X_n, \ n \geq 1\}$. Under very mild conditions the process has a limiting or steady-state distribution. These conditions are technical in nature and will be discussed later on in Section 3.7. The main

point, however, is that virtually any discrete time parameter regenerative

process of practical interest to a simulator has a steady-state distribution

in some sense, and most often in the following familiar sense. There is a

random K-vector $\underset{\sim}{X}$ such that the distribution of $\underset{\sim}{X}_n$ converges to the dis-

tribution of $\underset{\sim}{X}$ as $n \to \infty$, that is, the $\lim_{n \to \infty} P\{\underset{\sim}{X}_n \leq \underset{\sim}{x}\} = P\{\underset{\sim}{X} \leq \underset{\sim}{x}\}$. We

express this in a compact form by writing

$$\underset{\sim}{X}_n \Longrightarrow \underset{\sim}{X} \quad \text{as} \quad n \to \infty \quad . \tag{3.1}$$

An alternate type of convergence applies when $\underset{\sim}{X}_n$ is "periodic," and this

will be discussed in Section 3.7.

Since we now know that regenerative simulations of interest have

steady-state distributions, we can turn to the question of estimating character-

istics of those steady-state distributions.

Let f be a "nice" function in K dimensions having real values, and

suppose the goal of the simulation is to estimate the value of $r \equiv E\{f(\underset{\sim}{X})\}$.

(The "nice" functions are the so-called "measurable" functions, and these in-

clude virtually all functions of practical interest.) Now, by the appropriate

choice of the function f , the simulator can estimate a wide variety of

steady-state quantities of interest. To illustrate, suppose first that $\underset{\sim}{X}$ is

real-valued, so that we replace $\underset{\sim}{X}$ by X . If f is defined so that

$f(x) = x$ for all x , then $r \equiv E\{f(X)\} = E\{X\}$, so that estimating r is

equivalent to estimating $E\{X\}$. If $f(x) = x^2$, then $r = E\{X^2\}$; if

$f(x) = 1$ for $x \leq a$, where   a   is fixed, and $f(x) = 0$ for $x > a$,

then $r = P\{X \leq a\}$; and, if $f(x) = b(x - c)^+$, where   b   and   c   are fixed,

then $r = b \cdot E\{(X - c)^+\}$.

More generally, if x_j is the   jth   component of the K-vector $\underset{\sim}{x}$ and

$x^{(j)}$ is the   jth   component of $\underset{\sim}{X}$, then $f(\underset{\sim}{x}) = x_j$ gives $r = E\{x^{(j)}\}$,

$f(\underset{\sim}{x}) = x_i x_j$ gives $r = E\{x^{(i)}x^{(j)}\}$, and $f(\underset{\sim}{x}) = \left[x_1^2 + \ldots + x_k^2\right]^{\frac{1}{2}}$ gives

r   equal to the expected length in   K dimensions of the random vector $\underset{\sim}{X}$.
The reader should check which functions were used in the queueing and inventory
examples.

We now observe those properties of the regenerative structure which will
be used to obtain a confidence interval for   r . Let

$$Y_j = \sum_{i=\beta_j}^{\beta_{j+1}-1} f(\underset{\sim}{X}_i) . \tag{3.2}$$

That is, Y_j is the sum of the values of $f(\underset{\sim}{X}_i)$ over the   jth   cycle.
Recall that $\alpha_j = \beta_{j+1} - \beta_j$ gives the length of the   jth   cycle. Then, the
fundamental properties of the regenerative process we shall use are given by
(3.3) and (3.4).

The sequence $\{(Y_j, \alpha_j), j > 1\}$ consists of

independent and identically distributed random   (3.3)

vectors.

$\underline{\text{If}}$ $E\{|f(\underset{\sim}{X})|\} < \infty$ $\underline{\text{then}}$

$$r \equiv E\{f(\underset{\sim}{X})\} = E\{Y_1\}/E\{\alpha_1\} \ . \tag{3.4}$$

Note that we demonstrated the validity of (3.3) and (3.4) in the queueing and inventory examples. Let us now generalize the concepts which we used in those examples. We know that (3.3) holds since the vectors $\{(Y_j, \alpha_j), j > 1\}$ are defined in successive regeneration cycles, and these cycles are independent and exhibit the same probabilistic behavior. As for (3.4), it is known that under quite general conditions

$$\frac{f(\underset{\sim}{X}_1) + \ldots + f(\underset{\sim}{X}_N)}{N} \longrightarrow E\{f(\underset{\sim}{X})\} \tag{3.5}$$

as $N \to \infty$, with probability one. Now suppose that $\beta_1 = 1$ so that the first regeneration cycle starts at the very beginning of the simulation. If the nth cycle is completed at time N , then the ratio in (3.5) can be written as

$$\frac{(Y_1 + \ldots + Y_n)/n}{(\alpha_1 + \ldots + \alpha_n)/n} \ , \tag{3.6}$$

since Y_j is the sum of $f(\underset{\sim}{X}_i)$ in the jth cycle and α_j is the length of the jth cycle. But the ratio in (3.6) converges to $E\{Y_1\}/E\{\alpha_1\}$ with probability one as $n \to \infty$, because of (3.3) and the law of large numbers. Since

$n \to \infty$ as $N \to \infty$, we thus have the general relation given by (3.4).

Note that in the case where $\beta_1 > 1$ (i.e., the first cycle does not start immediately), the ratio (3.6) must be replaced with

$$\frac{(Y_0 + Y_1 + \ldots + Y_n)/n}{(\alpha_0 + \alpha_1 + \ldots + \alpha_n)/n} \quad , \qquad (3.6)'$$

where α_0 and Y_0 represent an initial "transient" in the simulation and are defined by $\alpha_0 = \beta_1 - 1$ and $Y_0 = f(\underset{\sim}{X}_1) + \ldots + f(\underset{\sim}{X}_{\beta_1 - 1})$. The random variable α_0 will generally have a distribution different from $\alpha_j, j \geq 1$, and Y_0 will generally have a distribution different from $Y_j, j \geq 1$. However, for large n , Y_0 will be very small compared to $Y_1 + \ldots + Y_n$ and α_0 will be very small compared to $\alpha_1 + \ldots + \alpha_n$, so that the ratio in (3.6)' still converges to $E\{Y_1\}/E\{\alpha_1\}$, and again we see the validity of (3.4).

The assumption that $E\{|f(\underset{\sim}{X})|\} < \infty$ in (3.4) is not very restrictive, and does not pose an obstacle to application of the regenerative method.

Let us now return to the main problem of interest here, namely that of estimating the value of $E\{f(\underset{\sim}{X})\}$ based on the simulation output. In view of (3.3) and (3.4) this statistical estimation problem has been reduced to the following:

<u>Given the independent and identically distributed observations</u>

$\{(Y_j, \alpha_j), j \geq 1\}$, <u>estimate</u> $r \equiv E\{Y_1\}/E\{\alpha_1\}$. $\qquad (3.7)$

Moreover, because we now have independent and identically distributed observations, we can use results from classical statistics to estimate $E\{Y_1\}/E\{\alpha_1\}$. In particular, we can obtain a confidence interval for this quantity, and a method for doing so will be given in Section 3.3.

3.2   Regenerative Processes in Continuous Time

A regenerative process $\{\underset{\sim}{X}(t), t \geq 0\}$ in K dimensions is a stochastic process which starts afresh probabilistically at an increasing sequence $0 \leq R_1 < R_2 \ldots$ of random epochs on the time axis $[0, \infty)$. Thus, between any two consecutive regeneration epochs R_j and R_{j+1}, say, the portion $\{\underset{\sim}{X}(t), R_j \leq t < R_{j+1}\}$ is an independent and identically distributed replicate of the portion between any other two consecutive regeneration epochs. However, the portion of the process between epoch 0 and epoch R_1, while independent of the rest of the process, is allowed to have a different distribution.

Let $\gamma_j = R_{j+1} - R_j$, $j \geq 1$. Then the sequence $\{\gamma_j, j \geq 1\}$ represents the time spans between consecutive epochs of regeneration, and is a sequence of independent and identically distributed variables. As before we make the mild assumption that $E\{\gamma_1\} < \infty$. This assumption is certainly satisfied for the repairman model of Section 2, and is also satisfied for any Markov chain in continuous time which is positive recurrent and irreducible.

For simulation applications it will be assumed that the process $\{\underset{\sim}{X}(t), t \geq 0\}$ has sample paths which are continuous from the right and make only a finite number of jumps in each finite time interval. These assumptions certainly hold in the repair model of Section 2, and are, in general, very mild assumptions for discrete-event simulations.

Just as in the case of regenerative processes in discrete time, it is true that regenerative processes in continuous time have limiting or steady-state distributions under very mild conditions. The exact conditions will be discussed in Section 3.7. Once again, however, the point is that virtually all regenerative processes of practical interest for simulation applications have steady-state distributions, and most often in the following sense. There is a random K-vector $\underset{\sim}{X}$ such that the distribution of $\underset{\sim}{X}(t)$ converges to the distribution of $\underset{\sim}{X}$ as $t \to \infty$. Following (3.1), we express this by writing

$$\underset{\sim}{X}(t) \implies \underset{\sim}{X} \qquad \text{as} \quad t \to \infty . \tag{3.8}$$

Now, let f be a "nice" function in K dimensions taking real values, and suppose the goal of the simulation is to estimate the value of $r \equiv E\{f(\underset{\sim}{X})\}$. For $j \geq 1$, let

$$Z_j = \int_{R_j}^{R_{j+1}} f[\underset{\sim}{X}(t)] \, dt ,$$

that is, Z_j is the integral of $f[\underset{\sim}{X}(t)]$ over the jth regeneration cycle. The following results are analogous to (3.3) and (3.4):

<u>The sequence</u> $\{(Z_j, \gamma_j), j \geq 1\}$ <u>consists of</u>
<u>independent and identically distributed random</u>   (3.9)
<u>vectors</u>.

<u>If</u> $E\{|f(\underset{\sim}{X})|\} < \infty$ <u>then</u>
                                                              (3.10)
$\quad$ $r \equiv E\{f(\underset{\sim}{X})\} = E\{Z_1\}/E\{\gamma_1\}$.

Note that we demonstrated the validity of (3.9) and (3.10) for the
repairman model of Section 2. The basic concepts which establish (3.9) and
(3.10) in a more general setting are the same as for the discrete-time case
in (3.3) and (3.4). As before, the condition that $E\{|f(\underset{\sim}{X})|\} < \infty$ is not
restrictive for applications.

By virtue of (3.9) and (3.10), the problem of estimating $E\{f(\underset{\sim}{X})\}$
has been reduced to that of estimating $E\{Z_1\}/E\{\gamma_1\}$ based on the independent
and identically distributed observations $\{(Z_j, \gamma_j), j \geq 1\}$. That is, we
have a problem in classical statistics identical to that given by (3.7) in
the discrete-time case, so that the same estimation methods (to be given in
Section 3.3) will apply in either case.

As a final note, the random variable Z_j is defined above as the
integral of $f[\underset{\sim}{X}(t)]$ over the interval from R_j to R_{j+1} . If we denote
by $t_1, t_2, \ldots t_m$, say, the time points in the interval from R_j to R_{j+1}
where the process has a "jump" and we let $t_0 = R_j$ and $t_{m+1} = R_{j+1}$, then

$$Z_j = \sum_{i=0}^{m} \int_{t_i}^{t_{i+1}} f[\underset{\sim}{X}(t)]\, dt$$

and each of the integrals in the above sum is usually easy to compute. For example, in the repairman model óf Section 2, the points $t_0, t_1, \ldots t_{m+1}$ represent the times (during the jth regeneration cycle) when the number of units at the repair facility goes up or down by one, i.e., a recently failed unit arrives or a repaired unit departs. In this particular case the process occupies the same state between successive jump times, so that the value of Z_j is simply the sum

$$\sum_{i=0}^{m} f[X(t_i)] \cdot (t_{i+1} - t_i) \; .$$

3.3   Confidence Intervals

We will now indicate how (3.3), (3.4), (3.9) and (3.10) can be used to obtain a confidence interval for $r \equiv E\{f(\underset{\sim}{X})\}$. The results will be stated for the discrete-time case, but they apply verbatim to the continuous-time case with Y_j replaced by Z_j and α_j replaced by γ_j .

In view of (3.7), we have the following task: given the independent and identically distributed pairs (Y_1, α_1) , $(Y_2, \alpha_2), \ldots (Y_n, \alpha_n)$, construct a $100(1 - \delta)\%$ confidence interval for $E\{Y_1\}/E\{\alpha_1\}$ when n is large. We illustrate one method for obtaining such a confidence interval using the central limit theorem. Further discussion of some alternate confidence intervals, and of various point estimators of r , will be given in Section 7.

Let $V_j = Y_j - r\alpha_j$. Note that the V_j's are independent and identically distributed and that $E\{V_j\} = E\{Y_j\} - r E\{\alpha_j\} = 0$, by virtue of (3.3)

and (3.4). Let $\overline{Y}$, $\overline{\alpha}$, and $\overline{V}$ denote the sample means

$$\overline{Y} = \frac{1}{n} \sum_{j=1}^{n} Y_j \quad ,$$

$$\overline{\alpha} = \frac{1}{n} \sum_{j=1}^{n} \alpha_j \quad ,$$

and

$$\overline{V} = \frac{1}{n} \sum_{j=1}^{n} V_j \quad ,$$

and note that $\overline{V} = \overline{Y} - r\overline{\alpha}$. Putting $\sigma^2 = E\{V_j^2\}$ and assuming $0 < \sigma^2 < \infty$, the central limit theorem tells us that

$$\lim_{n \to \infty} P \left\{ \frac{n^{1/2} \overline{V}}{\sigma} \leq x \right\} = \Phi(x) \tag{3.11}$$

for each real x , where Φ is the standard normal distribution function.
The assumption that $0 < \sigma^2 < \infty$ is not restrictive for simulation applications.
Now, from (3.11) we have

$$\lim_{n \to \infty} P \left\{ \frac{n^{1/2} [\overline{Y} - r\overline{\alpha}]}{\sigma} \leq x \right\} = \Phi(x)$$

which may be rewritten as

$$\lim_{n \to \infty} P \left\{ \frac{n^{1/2}[\hat{r} - r]}{(\sigma/\bar{\alpha})} \leq x \right\} = \Phi(x) \tag{3.12}$$

where $\hat{r} = \bar{Y}/\bar{\alpha}$. We cannot, however, produce a confidence interval for r directly from (3.12) since the value of σ is unknown. However, we can estimate the value of σ as follows. Note that

$$\sigma^2 = E\{(Y_1 - r\alpha_1)^2\} = Var\{Y_1\} - 2r \; Cov(Y_1, \alpha_1) + r^2 \; Var\{\alpha_1\} \; .$$

Let s_{11}, s_{22} and s_{12} denote, respectively, the sample variance of the Y_j's , the sample variance of the α_j's , and the sample covariance of the (Y_j, α_j)'s , i.e.,

$$s_{11} = \frac{1}{n-1} \sum_{j=1}^{n} (Y_j - \bar{Y})^2 = \frac{1}{n-1} \sum_{j=1}^{n} Y_j^2 - \frac{1}{n(n-1)} \left(\sum_{j=1}^{n} Y_j \right)^2 .$$

$$s_{22} = \frac{1}{n-1} \sum_{j=1}^{n} (\alpha_j - \bar{\alpha})^2 = \frac{1}{n-1} \sum_{j=1}^{n} \alpha_j^2 - \frac{1}{n(n-1)} \left(\sum_{j=1}^{n} \alpha_j \right)^2$$

and

$$s_{12} = \frac{1}{n-1} \sum_{j=1}^{n} (Y_j - \bar{Y})(\alpha_j - \bar{\alpha}) = \frac{1}{n-1} \sum_{j=1}^{n} Y_j \alpha_j - \frac{1}{n(n-1)} \left(\sum_{j=1}^{n} Y_j \right) \left(\sum_{j=1}^{n} \alpha_j \right)$$

Now let

$$s^2 = s_{11} - 2\hat{r}\,s_{12} + \hat{r}^2 s_{22} \; .$$

Then, it can be easily shown that $s^2 \to \sigma^2$ with probability one as $n \to \infty$. Thus, (3.12) holds with s in place of σ , i.e.,

$$\lim_{n\to\infty} P\left\{\frac{n^{1/2}[\hat{r} - r]}{(s/\overline{\alpha})} \leq x\right\} = \Phi(x) \; . \tag{3.13}$$

Letting $z_\delta^* = \Phi^{-1}(1 - \frac{\delta}{2})$, i.e., $\Phi(z_\delta^*) = 1 - \frac{\delta}{2}$, then from (3.13) we have

$$P\left\{- z_\delta^* \leq \frac{n^{1/2}[\hat{r} - r]}{(s/\overline{\alpha})} \leq z_\delta^*\right\} \cong 1 - \delta$$

for large n . This may be rewritten as

$$P\left\{\hat{r} - \frac{z_\delta^* s}{\overline{\alpha}\,n^{1/2}} \leq r \leq \hat{r} + \frac{z_\delta^* s}{\overline{\alpha}\,n^{1/2}}\right\} \cong 1 - \delta \; ,$$

giving the following approximate $100(1 - \delta)\%$ confidence interval for

$r = E\{f(\underset{\sim}{X})\}$:

$$\hat{I} = \left[\hat{r} - \frac{z_\delta^* s}{\bar{\alpha}\, n^{1/2}} \quad , \quad \hat{r} + \frac{z_\delta^* s}{\bar{\alpha}\, n^{1/2}} \right] \tag{3.14}$$

Note that if we let $\hat{J}$ be the width of $\hat{I}$, then

$$\hat{J} \cong \frac{2\, z_\delta^*\, \sigma}{E\{\alpha_1\} n^{1/2}}$$

for large n , with high probability. Thus, in order to reduce the width of the confidence interval $\hat{I}$ by a factor of two (at the same level of confidence), it is necessary to increase the number of cycles simulated by a factor of four.

We now summarize the procedure for obtaining an approximate $100(1 - \delta)\%$ confidence interval for $r = E\{f(\underset{\sim}{X})\}$:

1. Observe the simulation for n regeneration cycles.

2. Compute Y_j and α_j for each cycle j , where Y_j is the sum of $f(\underset{\sim}{X}_i)$ over the jth cycle and α_j is the length of the jth cycle.

3. Compute the sample statistics[1]

$$\bar{Y} = \frac{1}{n} \sum_{j=1}^{n} Y_j \quad , \quad \bar{\alpha} = \frac{1}{n} \sum_{j=1}^{n} \alpha_j \quad , \quad \hat{r} = \bar{Y}/\bar{\alpha}$$

---

[1]In performing these calculations, particularly those of s_{11}, s_{12}, and s_{22}, it is wise to use <u>double-precision</u> arithmetic in order to insure the desired degree of accuracy in computing the sums.

$$s_{11} = \frac{1}{n-1} \sum_{j=1}^{n} Y_j^2 - \frac{1}{n(n-1)} \left(\sum_{j=1}^{n} Y_j \right)^2, \quad s_{22} = \frac{1}{n-1} \sum_{j=1}^{n} \alpha_j^2 - \frac{1}{n(n-1)} \left(\sum_{j=1}^{n} \alpha_j \right)^2,$$

$$s_{12} = \frac{1}{n-1} \sum_{j=1}^{n} Y_j \alpha_j - \frac{1}{n(n-1)} \left(\sum_{j=1}^{n} Y_j \right) \left(\sum_{j=1}^{n} \alpha_j \right),$$

$$s^2 = s_{11} - 2\hat{r} s_{12} + \hat{r}^2 s_{22}.$$

4. **Form** the confidence interval

$$\hat{r} \pm \frac{z_\delta^* s}{\bar{\alpha} n^{1/2}}$$

where $z_\delta^* = \Phi^{-1}(1 - \frac{\delta}{2})$ and Φ is the standard normal distribution function.

Note that in the case where the first cycle does not begin immediately at the start of the simulation, the above procedure indicates that the data prior to the first cycle is to be discarded.

In order to clarify the procedure that has just been summarized, let us follow through this procedure for a numerical example.

Example. Suppose a simulator desires to obtain a 90% confidence interval for $E\{W\}$, the mean customer waiting time in steady-state, from a queueing simulation.

The simulator executes a single simulation run of the model and observes the following customer waiting times:

$W_1 = 0$ $W_{11} = 0$ $W_{21} = 10$ $W_{31} = 16$ $W_{41} = 0$

$W_2 = 10$ $W_{12} = 12$ $W_{22} = 8$ $W_{32} = 4$

$W_3 = 8$ $W_{13} = 9$ $W_{23} = 14$ $W_{33} = 0$

$W_4 = 15$ $W_{14} = 18$ $W_{24} = 14$ $W_{34} = 8$

$W_5 = 17$ $W_{15} = 18$ $W_{25} = 13$ $W_{35} = 18$

$W_6 = 13$ $W_{16} = 10$ $W_{26} = 10$ $W_{36} = 12$

$W_7 = 18$ $W_{17} = 0$ $W_{27} = 8$ $W_{37} = 18$

$W_8 = 12$ $W_{18} = 16$ $W_{28} = 12$ $W_{38} = 19$

$W_9 = 2$ $W_{19} = 0$ $W_{29} = 13$ $W_{39} = 8$

$W_{10} = 5$ $W_{20} = 5$ $W_{30} = 23$ $W_{40} = 4$

1. In this run there are $n = 5$ cycles, which are initiated by customers 1, 11, 17, 19, and 33.

2. $\alpha_1 = 10$ $Y_1 = \sum_{i=1}^{10} W_i = 100$

$\alpha_2 = 6$ $Y_2 = \sum_{i=11}^{16} W_i = 67$

$\alpha_3 = 2$ $Y_3 = \sum_{i=17}^{18} W_i = 16$

$$\alpha_4 = 14 \qquad Y_4 = \sum_{i=19}^{32} W_i = 150$$

$$\alpha_5 = 8 \qquad Y_5 = \sum_{i=33}^{40} W_i = 87$$

3. $\bar{Y} = \dfrac{1}{5} \displaystyle\sum_{j=1}^{5} Y_j = 84$, $\bar{\alpha} = \dfrac{1}{5} \displaystyle\sum_{j=1}^{5} \alpha_j = 8$, $\hat{r} = \bar{Y}/\bar{\alpha} = 10.5$,

$$s_{11} = \frac{1}{4} \sum_{j=1}^{5} Y_j^2 - \frac{1}{20} \left(\sum_{j=1}^{5} Y_j \right)^2 = 2383.5$$

$$s_{22} = \frac{1}{4} \sum_{j=1}^{5} \alpha_j^2 - \frac{1}{20} \left(\sum_{j=1}^{5} \alpha_j \right)^2 = 20 \quad ,$$

$$s_{12} = \frac{1}{4} \sum_{j=1}^{5} Y_j \alpha_j - \frac{1}{20} \left(\sum_{j=1}^{5} Y_j \right) \left(\sum_{j=1}^{5} \alpha_j \right) = 217.5$$

$$s^2 = s_{11} - 2\hat{r} s_{12} + \hat{r}^2 s_{22} = 21 \quad .$$

4. Confidence interval (90%) is

$$\hat{I} = \hat{r} \pm \frac{z_{0.1}^* s}{\bar{\alpha} n^{1/2}} = 10.5 \pm \frac{(1.645)(21)^{1/2}}{8(5)^{1/2}} = 10.5 \pm 0.4214$$

The width of $\hat{I}$ is 0.8428 , and reducing this width by a factor of two (at 90% confidence) would require about 20 cycles.

3.4   Sample Simulation Results for Models of Section 2

    We now present sample simulation results for the queueing, inventory, and repairman models of Section 2. The results were obtained using the regenerative approach; in particular, confidence intervals for the various steady-state parameters were computed using the technique given in Section 3.3. We first present results for the queueing model.

    Recall that we have a standard single-server queueing system (as depicted in Figure 2.1) in which the interarrival times are constant with value 60 and the service times are uniformly distributed on $[10, 90]$. We are interested in $E\{W\}$ where W is the steady-state waiting time. We estimate $E\{W\}$ (and other characteristics of W as well) by simulating the customer waiting times W_1, W_2, . . . and analyzing the output. The sequence $\{W_n, n \geq 1\}$ is a regenerative process in discrete time, and regeneration occurs at time n (i.e., with customer n) if $W_n = 0$. For the simulation, we set $W_1 = 0$, $\beta_1 = 1$, and let β_{k+1} be the index of the $(k + 1)$st customer whose waiting time is zero, for k = 1, 2, ... Then, we let $\alpha_1 = \beta_2 - \beta_1$, . . . , $\alpha_k = \beta_{k+1} - \beta_k$, ... We refer to α_k as the length of the kth cycle. In other words, α_k is the number of customers served in the kth busy period.

    Table 3.1 presents simulation results for the queueing model based on a run of 1500 observed cycles. Confidence intervals at the 95% level are given for the parameters $E\{W\}$, $E\{W^2\}$, $E\{(W - 24)^+\}$, $P\{W > 24\}$, and $P\{\alpha_1 > 6\}$. Confidence intervals are computed using the formulas of Section 3.3.

Note, it can be shown theoretically that, for this particular model, $E\{W\} \leq 23.667$ and $E\{\alpha_1\} \leq 5.208$. Thus, we might regard $E\{(W - 24)^+\}$ as a "penalty" for long waiting times, $P\{W > 24\}$ as the likelihood of a long waiting time, and $P\{\alpha > 6\}$ as the likelihood of a long busy period.

Table 3.1 - <u>Simulation Results for Queueing Model</u>
(run length = 1500 cycles, level of confidence = 95%)

Parameter	Confidence Interval
$E\{W\}$	[13.303, 17.128]
$E\{W^2\}$	[499.700, 885.420]
$E\{(W - 24)^+\}$	[4.014, 6.754]
$P\{W > 24\}$	[0.229, 0.287]
$P\{\alpha > 6\}$	[0.047, 0.071]
$E\{\alpha_1\}$	[2.122, 2.399]

We next consider the inventory model. In this system, the demand for an item in a period has a binomial distribution with parameters 9 and 1/3. The inventory level of the item is checked at the beginning of each period. If fewer than 3 units are on hand, an order is placed which immediately raises the inventory level to 7 units; otherwise, no order is placed. We are interested in the parameters $E\{X\}$ and $E\{\min(X,D)\}$ where X is the steady-state number of units on hand at the beginning of a period immediately after the ordering decision has been made and D is the demand for the item in the ensuing period. We estimate these steady-state parameters (and others as well) by simulating the post-ordering-decision inventory levels X_1, X_2, . . . and analyzing the output. The sequence $\{X_n, n \geq 1\}$ is a regenerative process in discrete time, and regeneration occurs at time n (i.e., at period n) if $X_n = 7$. For the simulation, we set $X_1 = 7$, $\beta_1 = 1$, and then let β_{k+1} be the number of the $(k+1)$st period in which the post-ordering-decision inventory level is 7, for $k = 1, 2, ...$ We let $\alpha_1 = \beta_2 - \beta_1, . . . , \alpha_k = \beta_{k+1} - \beta_k, . . . ,$ and call α_k the length of the kth cycle.

Table 3.2 presents simulation results for the inventory system based on a run of 300 observed cycles. Theoretical values and 95% confidence intervals are given for the parameters $E\{X\}$, $E\{\min(X,D)\}$, $E\{\alpha_1\}$, and π_j where $\pi_j = P\{X = j\}$ for $j = 3, 4, 5, 6, 7$.

Finally, we consider the repairman model. Recall that we have a system as depicted in Figure 2.3 with 10 operating units, 5 spare units, and 4 servers at the repair facility. The "lifetime" of an operating unit is exponentially distributed with mean 5, and the time required to repair a unit is exponentially distributed with mean 2. We are interested in the parameters $E\{(X - 5)^+\}$ and

Table 3.2 <u>Simulation Results for Inventory System</u>
(run length = 300 cycles, level of confidence = 95%)

Parameter	Theoretical Value	Confidence Interval
$E\{X\}$	5.528	[5.487, 5.624]
$E\{\min(X, D)\}$	2.870	[2.811, 3.000]
$E\{\alpha_1\}$	2.061	[1.942, 2.078]
π_3	0.168	[0.143, 0.192]
π_4	0.165	[0.136, 0.189]
π_5	0.124	[0.092, 0.137]
π_6	0.058	[0.040, 0.076]
π_7	0.485	[0.481, 0.514]

$P\{X > 5\}$ where X is the number of units at the repair facility (waiting for and undergoing repair) under steady-state conditions. We estimate these steady-state parameters (and others as well) by simulating the process $\{X(t), t \geq 0\}$, where $X(t)$ is the number of units at the repair facility at time t . The process $\{X(t), t \geq 0\}$ is a regenerative process in continuous time, and regeneration occurs at time t if the repair facility becomes completely idle at t . For the simulation, we put $X(0) = 0$, $R_1 = 0$, and then let R_{k+1} be the time of the $(k + 1)$st entrance to state 0 by the process $\{X(t), t \geq 0\}$. We then let $\gamma_1 = R_2 - R_1$, . . . , $\gamma_{k+1} = R_{k+1} - R_k$, for $k = 1, 2, \ldots$. We refer to γ_k as the duration of the kth cycle. Also, we let $\hat{\gamma}_k$ be the number of failures over the kth cycle.

Table 3.3 gives simulation results for the repairman model based on a run of 500 observed cycles. Theoretical values and 95% confidence intervals are given for the parameters $E\{X\}$, $E\{(X - 5)^+\}$, $P\{X > 5\}$, $P\{X > 0\}$, $P\{X = 0\}$, $E\{\gamma_1\}$, and $E\{\hat{\gamma}_1\}$.

Table 3.3 Simulation Results for Repair Model
(run length = 500 cycles, level of confidence = 95%)

Parameter	Theoretical Value	Confidence Interval
$E\{X\}$	5.353	[5.238, 5.432]
$E\{(X - 5)^+\}$	1.269	[1.201, 1.325]
$P\{X > 5\}$	0.465	[0.444, 0.475]
$P\{X > 0\}$	0.988	[0.987, 0.990]
$P\{X = 0\}$	0.012	[0.010, 0.013]
$E\{\gamma_1\}$	42.021	[37.459, 47.681]
$E\{\hat{\gamma}_1\}$	73.375	[65.262, 83.342]

3.5   Tactical Questions

We now discuss the questions of simulation run length in the context of regenerative simulations. We also show how the regenerative approach can be used in cases where a fixed-length simulation is desired (rather than a fixed number of cycles). Finally, we discuss selection of the regenerative points in the case where a simulation may have two or more possible choices for such regeneration points.

Let us first consider the problem of determining run length. The $100(1 - \delta)\%$ confidence interval obtained in Section 3.3, for a simulation run with a fixed number of cycles n, has a width which is approximately

$$\frac{w \, \Phi^{-1}(1 - \frac{\delta}{2})}{n^{1/2}}$$

for large n, where $w = 2\sigma/E\{\alpha_1\}$. (In the continuous-time case $w = 2\sigma/E\{\gamma_1\}$.) Note that since σ is unknown, w is also unknown prior to the simulation. Also, the expected cycle length $E\{\alpha_1\}$ is unknown in advance. Hence, the simulator may wish to make a small "pilot" run to obtain a rough estimate for w and for $E\{\alpha_1\}$. Such an estimate would be of help in determining the ultimate run length and level of confidence, with the appropriate tradeoff between cost of sampling (computer time) and the degree of precision desired (i.e., level of confidence and width of confidence interval).

Now note that the procedure given in Section 3.3 for obtaining a confidence interval for $r \equiv E\{f(\underline{X})\}$ requires that statistics be gathered over a fixed number of regeneration cycles, so that the actual run length of the simulation is not fixed in advance. Alternatively, it is possible to perform a similar analysis for a simulation run of fixed length t . Let $N(t)$ denote the number of complete regeneration cycles observed by time t , that is,

$$N(t) = n \quad \text{if } \beta_n \leq t < \beta_{n+1} \quad .$$

Now redefine all the sample statistics by replacing n with $N(t)$. Based on the central limit theorem for partial sums with a random number of terms, it follows that (3.13) continues to hold, with n replaced by $N(t)$, as $t \to \infty$. Consequently, for large t , (3.14) provides an approximate $100(1 - \delta)\%$ confidence interval for $E\{f(\underset{\sim}{X})\}$, again with the substitution of $N(t)$ for n. In other words, the procedure for a fixed run length t is identical to the procedure for a fixed number of regeneration cycles, except that statistics are computed only for the cycles completed by time t .

It is known that the ratio $N(t) \cdot E\{\alpha_1\}/t$ converges to the value 1 as $t \to \infty$, with probability one. Thus, replacing $N(t)$ by $t/E\{\alpha_1\}$, we see that the confidence interval obtained in the manner above for a run of fixed duration t has a length which is approximately

$$\frac{d \, \Phi^{-1}(1 - \frac{\delta}{2})}{t^{1/2}}$$

for large t,, where $d = 2\sigma/[E\{\alpha_1\}]^{1/2}$. Again, since σ is unknown, d is also unknown prior to the simulation. Hence, the simulator may want to take a small sample to obtain a rough estimate for d . As before, such an estimate would form a basis for a final decision on run length and level of confidence.

We now turn to the question of choice of regeneration points. In the queueing example of Section 2, the state space for $\{W_n, n \geq 1\}$ is $[0, \infty)$ but state "0" is the only return or regeneration state. In the repairman model, however, the state space of $\{X(t), t \geq 0\}$ is $\{0, 1, 2, \ldots, 15\}$ and since the repair times are exponentially distributed, each of the states can serve as a regeneration state. (In fact, the process $\{X(t), t \geq 0\}$ is a positive recurrent, irreducible Markov chain with a continuous time para-meter.) In the inventory example we chose state 7 as the return state. But the post-ordering-decision inventory levels $\{X_n, n \geq 1\}$ can be any one of 3, 4, 5, 6, 7, and, owing to the nature of the demands, the times of successive returns to any one of these states can serve as regeneration points. Thus, for example, we can say that n is an epoch of regeneration if $X_n = 4$, group the output into blocks according to successive returns to state 4 and proceed to construct confidence intervals for $E\{X\}$ and $E\{\min(X, D)\}$ by the procedure given earlier. Now, a natural question for the simulator to ask is how the lengths of the confidence intervals vary for the different return states 7 and 4 . Indeed, the same question arises in the simulation of any positive recurrent irreducible Markov chain, since each state can serve as a return state. Fortunately, the question has a simple answer which we frame in the following way.

Suppose the regenerative process, say $\{\underset{\sim}{X}_n, n \geq 1\}$, has two sequences $\{\beta_j, j \geq 1\}$ and $\{\beta'_j, j \geq 1\}$ of regeneration times. Let

$$\alpha_j = \beta_{j+1} - \beta_j \quad , \quad \alpha'_j = \beta'_{j+1} - \beta'_j \quad ,$$

$$Y_j = \sum_{n=\beta_j}^{\beta_{j+1}-1} f(\underset{\sim}{X}_n)$$

and

$$Y'_j = \sum_{n=\beta'_j}^{\beta'_{j+1}-1} f(\underset{\sim}{X}_n) \quad .$$

Based on the sequences $\{(Y_j, \alpha_j), j \geq 1\}$ and $\{(Y'_j, \alpha'_j), j \geq 1\}$ and a simulation run of length t , suppose the simulator can construct confidence intervals of lengths $I(t)$ and $I'(t)$, respectively, for $r = E\{f(\underset{\sim}{X})\}$. **Then,** it can be shown that, **with probability one,**

$$\lim_{t \to \infty} \frac{I(t)}{I'(t)} = 1$$

Thus, if the simulator has the choice of two or more regenerative sequences (resulting, say, from two or more return states) on which to base his confidence interval, then with high probability the lengths of the resulting confidence intervals will be approximately equal when the length t of the simulation run is large. The simulator may therefore pick which-ever sequence (or return state) is most convenient.

3.6   Cost Structures

Frequently a simulator may be more interested in estimating the average per unit time of some "cost" function associated with his simulation than in functions of the stationary distribution. Suppose the cost per unit time associated with the regenerative process being in state $\underset{\sim}{y}$ is $f(\underset{\sim}{y})$ where f is a "nice" function. Then the average cost per unit time over the interval [0, t] is

$$\frac{1}{t} \int_0^t f[\underset{\sim}{X}(s)]\, ds \quad .$$

Under the same mild conditions which lead to (3.8) and (3.10), we have that

$$\lim_{t \to \infty} \frac{1}{t} \int_0^t f[\underset{\sim}{X}(s)]\, ds \;=\; E\{f(\underset{\sim}{X})\} \tag{3.15}$$

with probability one. Thus, we see that by estimating $E\{f(\underset{\sim}{X})\}$, we also obtain an estimate for the asymptotic cost per unit time.

The above approach may be generalized to include virtually any cost structure on the simulation which accumulates costs based on the simulatiion transitions and the times spent in each state. This is so because such costs can be divided into independent and identically distributed pieces associated with each regeneration cycle. To illustrate one such general cost structure, suppose the regenerative process $\{X(s), \ s \geq 0\}$ changes state at the random times $\{t_n, \ n \geq 1\}$, and let $S(t)$ denote the number of changes of state in the interval $[0, \ t]$. The cost structure we consider has two components: if the process changes state from x to y , the cost of this change is $f_1(x, \ y)$; and, if the process is in state y , at a time s units after a change of state and the last state was x , then the cost per unit time is $f_2(x, \ y, \ s)$. Letting $C(t; \ f_1, \ f_2)$ denote the total cost in $[0, \ t]$, we have

$$C(t; \ f_1 \ f_2) \ = \ \sum_{n=1}^{S(t)} f_1\Big[X(t_{n-1}), \ X(t_n)\Big]$$

$$+ \ \sum_{n=1}^{S(t)} \int_0^{t_n - t_{n-1}} f_2\Big[X(t_{n-2}), \ X(t_{n-1}), \ s\Big] \, ds$$

$$+ \ \int_0^{t - t_{S(t)}} f_2\Big[X(t_{S(t)-1}), \ X(t_{S(t)}), \ s\Big] \, ds$$

where $t_{-1} = t_0 = 0$. Let $Y_j(f_1, \ f_2) = C(\beta_{j+1}; \ f_1, \ f_2) - C(\beta_j; \ f_1, \ f_2)$; that is, $Y_j(f_1, \ f_2)$ is the total cost accumulated in the jth regeneration cycle. Note that the Y_j's form a sequence of independent and identically distributed random variables. Then, under mild conditions, we have

$$\lim_{t \to \infty} \frac{1}{t} \cdot C(t; f_1, f_2) = E\{Y_1(f_1, f_2)\}/E\{\alpha_1\} \qquad (3.16)$$

with probability one. The arguments used in establishing (3.16) are similar to those used in establishing (3.4). Thus, upon estimating $E\{Y_1(f_1, f_2)\}/E\{\alpha_1\}$, we have an estimate for this more general cost per unit time. Moreover, this ratio estimation problem is identical to that discussed in Section 3.3.

3.7 Conditions Insuring Steady-State Distributions

In Sections 3.1 and 3.2 we stated the fact that under very mild conditions regenerative processes in both discrete and continuous time possess limiting or steady-state distributions. These conditions involve the distribution of the random variable α_1 in the discrete-time case and the distribution of γ_1 in the continuous-time case.

We first consider the discrete-time case. As before, we are assuming that $E\{\alpha_1\} < \infty$. Now, let $\varphi(k) = P\{\alpha_1 = k\}$ for $k = 1, 2, \ldots$. That is, φ is the probability mass function of the integer-valued random variable α_1. The function φ is said to be periodic with period h, where h is a positive integer, if

$$\sum_{k=1}^{\infty} \varphi(k\,h) = 1 \quad,$$

i.e., φ concentrates all of the probability on the integer multiples of h, so that α_1 can only take on such integer multiple values. If $h = 1$ then

φ is said to be aperiodic. The case most often encountered in simulation applications is that φ is aperiodic, and when this happens the regenerative process $\{\underset{\sim}{X}_n, n \geq 1\}$ has a steady-state distribution in the usual sense of (3.1). Moreover, φ is aperiodic whenever $\varphi(1) > 0$, a condition which is usually very easy to check. For example, in the queueing model of Section 2, $\varphi(1) = P\{\alpha_1 = 1\} = P\{W_2 = 0\} > 0$, since there is a positive probability that the first customer's service will be completed before the second customer arrives. And, in the inventory example, $P\{\alpha_1 = 1\} \geq P\{D_1 = 0\} > 0$. In those cases where $h > 1$, we have that (3.1) holds with $\underset{\sim}{X}_{nh}$ in place of $\underset{\sim}{X}_n$ and $n \to \infty$. Thus, the regenerative method can still be applied, but with the appropriate modifications; i.e., the ratio (3.4) becomes $h E\{Y_1\}/E\{\alpha_1\}$ and Y_k is the sum of $f(\underset{\sim}{X}_{ih})$ over the jth regeneration cycle, when $h > 1$. For the continuous-time case we also assume, as before, that $E\{\gamma_1\} < \infty$. Let F denote the distribution function of γ_1, i.e., $F(s) = P\{\gamma_1 \leq s\}$. The distribution function F is said to be arithmetic with span $\lambda > 0$ if the random variable γ_1 takes its values in the set $\{0, \lambda, 2\lambda, \ldots\}$ with probability one. Otherwise, F is said to be non-arithmetic. When F is non-arithmetic, the regenerative process $\{\underset{\sim}{X}(t), t \geq 0\}$ has a steady-state distribution in the usual sense of (3.8). Moreover, it is not hard to check if F is non-arithmetic. In the repairman model of Section 2, γ_1 is composed of the time, call it T_1, until the first failure in a "like-new" system plus the amount of time then required for the repair station to become completely idle. Since T_1 has an exponential distribution, and thus has a distribution function which is continuous, it follows that the distribution F of γ_1 is non-arithmetic.

In general, whenever γ_1 is built-up from at least one random variable having a continuous distribution function, the simulator can be assured that F is non-arithmetic. This will always be the case for any irreducible, positive recurrent Markov chain. In those cases where F is arithmetic with span λ , we have that (3.8) holds with t replaced by $n\lambda$ and $n \to \infty$; also, the ratio (3.10) becomes $\lambda E\{Z_1\}/E\{\gamma_1\}$ and Z_j is the sum of $f(\underset{\sim}{X}_{i\lambda})$ over the jth regeneration cycle.

4.0   MORE EXAMPLES OF REGENERATIVE PROCESSES

In this section we present three additional examples of stochastic
systems which have a regenerative structure in order to further the reader's
understanding of the regenerative approach. The first example considered is
an inventory distribution system for a single item that models an actual
system in current use. The second example is that of a "particles-in-a-box
Markov chain." Chains of this sort arise frequently in several applied contexts. The third example is that of a "Markov chain with a random time clock."
Processes of this type are the simplest and most important examples of Markov chains
with a finite number of states and a continuous time parameter. Sample simulation results using the regenerative approach are provided for each example.

4.1   An Inventory Distribution Model

We consider the following model of an inventory distribution
system for a single item. An inventory warehouse fills orders for two types
of customers: retail stores, ordering in large quantities; and direct customers, ordering at most a single unit at a time. Table 4.1 shows the ordering statistics for each of three retail stores. In addition to the lot size,
the table shows p_{sj} , the probability that j weeks transpire between orders
from store s . For example, if store 3 orders this week, the probability
is 1/4 that it will order again in 3 weeks, 1/2 in 4 weeks, and 1/4 in 5 weeks.
Given that it orders, the quantity ordered will be 50.

TABLE 4.1 Retail Store Ordering Statistics

Store s	Lot Size	Ordering Probabilities p_{sj}					
		$j = 1$	$j = 2$	$j = 3$	$j = 4$	$j = 5$	$j = 6$
1	40	0	$\frac{1}{8}$	$\frac{1}{4}$	$\frac{1}{4}$	$\frac{1}{4}$	$\frac{1}{8}$
2	30	0	$\frac{1}{5}$	$\frac{1}{5}$	$\frac{1}{5}$	$\frac{1}{5}$	$\frac{1}{5}$
3	50	0	0	$\frac{1}{4}$	$\frac{1}{2}$	$\frac{1}{4}$	0

In addition to the retail stores, there are 160 small customers who order directly from the warehouse. Each of these customers has a probability of $1/4$ of ordering in any given week, regardless of the length of time since the last order. The order quantity for each direct customer is one.

Suppose this inventory distribution system is to be simulated, and the simulation outputs to be observed are q_{ns} , the number of units ordered by store s in the nth week $(s = 1,2,3)$; and q_{n4} , the number of orders received from direct customers in the nth week. Let $\underset{\sim}{q}_n = (q_{n1}, q_{n2}, q_{n3}, q_{n4})$ and let β_k denote the kth time after the start of the simulation that $\underset{\sim}{q}_k \in A$, where

$$A = \{x \in R^4 : x_1 > 0 , x_2 > 0 , x_3 > 0\} .$$

That is, β_k is the kth time that all three stores place an order in the same week. Then, the times $\{\beta_k, k > 1\}$ are regeneration times for the process $\{q_n, n \geq 1\}$, and may be used to partition the output sequence into independent and identically distributed blocks as discussed in Section 3. Thus, we will be able to obtain confidence intervals for $E\{f(q)\}$ where q is the random vector to which q_n converges in distribution.

The following functions $f : R^4 \to (-\infty, \infty)$ are to be considered. For $x \in R^4$, let $y = $ (number of components of x_1, x_2, x_3 which are positive) and define:

$$f_1(x) = y + x_4$$

$$f_2(x) = x_1 + x_2 + x_3 + x_4$$

$$f_3(x) = (y + x_4)^2$$

$$f_4(x) = (x_1 + x_2 + x_3 + x_4)^2$$

$$f_5(x) = \begin{cases} 1, & x_1 + x_2 + x_3 + x_4 > 75 \\ 0, & x_1 + x_2 + x_3 + x_4 \leq 75 \end{cases}$$

$$f_6(x) = \begin{cases} 1, & x_1 > 0 \text{ and } x_2 > 0 \\ 0, & \text{otherwise} \end{cases}$$

$$f_7(x) = \begin{cases} 1, & x_1 = x_2 = x_3 = 0 \\ 0, & \text{otherwise} \end{cases}$$

$$f_8(\underset{\sim}{x}) = x_1 + x_2 + x_3$$

$$f_9(\underset{\sim}{x}) = 5 + .1(y + x_4) + .1(x_1 + x_2 + x_3 + x_4) + 100(x_1 + x_2 + x_3 + x_4)^{1/4} \ .$$

These functions are used, respectively, to estimate the expected number of orders in a week, the expected number of units ordered in a week, the second moment of the number of orders, the second moment of the number of units, the probability that more than 75 units are ordered in a week, the probability that both store # 1 and store # 2 place an order in a given week, the probability of no store orders in a week, the expected number of units ordered by stores in a week, and the expected value of a cost function on the warehouse operations. The cost function may be interperted as follows: a set cost of 5 per week, a requisition processing cost of .1 per order received, a material handling cost of .1 per unit ordered, and a transportation cost per unit ordered of $100 \cdot (\text{number of units})^{1/4}$.

Now let $\alpha_k = \beta_{k+1} - \beta_k$, and define

$$Y_k^{(i)} = \sum_{j=\beta_k}^{\beta_{k+1}-1} f_i(\underset{\sim}{q}) \ , \quad k \geq 1 \ , \quad i = 1, \ldots, 9 \ .$$

The sequences $\{(Y_k^{(i)}, \alpha_k) : k \geq 1\}$, $i = 1, \ldots, 9$, are independent and identically distributed by (3.3); and, by (3.4),

$$E\{f_i(\underset{\sim}{q})\} = E\{Y_1^{(i)}\} / E\{\alpha_1\} \ .$$

Thus, the statistical approach of Section 3 can be used to obtain confidence intervals for $E\{f_i(\underset{\sim}{q})\}$.

Table 4.2 shows the results of a simulation run for the above model. The level of confidence chosen was 95% and the length of run was 1,280 weeks. For this particular run, each of the confidence intervals obtained surrounded the theoretical parameter being estimated.

TABLE 4.2: <u>Simulation Results for the Inventory Model</u> (run length = 1,280 weeks, level of confidence = 95%)

Parameter	Theoretical Value	Confidence Interval
$E\{f_1(\underset{\sim}{q})\}$ = E{number of orders}	40.75	[40.35, 41.04]
$E\{f_2(\underset{\sim}{q})\}$ = E{number of units}	70.00	[69.80, 71.15]
$E\{f_3(\underset{\sim}{q})\}$ = E{(number of orders)^2}	1691.13	[1658.10, 1712.80]
$E\{f_4(\underset{\sim}{q})\}$ = E{(number of units)^2}	5867.50	[5815.21, 6051.32]
$E\{f_5(\underset{\sim}{q})\}$ = P{more than 75 units ordered}	.4351	[0.4207, 0.4650]
$E\{f_6(\underset{\sim}{q})\}$ = P{stores 1 and 2 both order}	.0625	[0.0480, 0.0775]
$E\{f_7(\underset{\sim}{q})\}$ = P{no stores order}	.4219	[0.3929, 0.4336]
$E\{f_8(\underset{\sim}{q})\}$ = E{number of units ordered by stores}	30.00	[29.99, 31.09]
$E\{f_9(\underset{\sim}{q})\}$ = E{warehouse operation cost}	300.02	[299.93, 301.86]

4.2   Particles-in-a-Box Markov Chain

An example of a Markov chain arising in several applied contexts is the following. Suppose C_n particles are added to a box at times $n = 1, 2, \ldots$, where C_n, $n \geq 1$, are independent and have a common Poisson distribution with parameter 1. Further, suppose that each particle in the box at time n , independently of all the other particles in the box and independently of how particles are added to the box, has probability $1/2$ of remaining in the box at time $n + 1$ and probability of $1/2$ of being removed from the box at time $n + 1$. Lex X_n denote the number of particles in the box at time n . The X_n's form a Markov chain with state space $\{0, 1, 2, \ldots\}$.

This same Markov chain can be used to describe a telephone exchange where C_n is the number of new calls starting at time n , the probability is $1/2$ that a call in progress at time n terminates by time $n + 1$, and X_n is the number of calls in progress at time n . This chain could also describe a large warehouse stocking many items where C_n is the number of new orders arriving at time n , the probability is $1/2$ that an order being processed at time n is filled by time $n + 1$, and X_n is the number of orders being processed at time n .

The type of Markov chain presented here is irreducible and aperiodic, and has a steady-state distribution in the sense of (3.1); i.e., there is a random variable X such that $P\{X_n = i\} \longrightarrow P\{X = i\}$ as $n \to \infty$ for each $i = 0, 1, 2, \ldots$.

For the simulation analysis we put $X_1 = 0$, $\beta_1 = 1$, and let β_k denote the time of the kth return to state 0 for $k > 1$. Then, of course, $\{\beta_1, \beta_2, \ldots\}$ is a sequence of regeneration times for $\{X_n, n \geq 1\}$ with return state 0 . The choice of 0 as return state is arbitrary. Table 4.3 shows results of a sample simulation of this Markov chain example. The run consisted of 1,000 cycles of returns to state 0 . Approximate 95% confidence intervals are given for various parameters. In each case the confidence interval obtained surrounded the true value of the parameter being estimated. The symbol π_i denotes $P\{X = i\}$, and $\alpha_k = \beta_{k+1} - \beta_k$.

TABLE 4.3 Simulation Results for Particles-in-a-Box Markov Chain
(run length = 1,000 cycles, level of confidence = 95%)

Parameter	Theoretical Value	Confidence Interval
$E\{X\}$	2.000	[1.963, 2.052]
$E\{X^2\}$	6.000	[5.713, 6.175]
π_0	0.135	[0.117, 0.137]
π_1	0.271	[0.260, 0.282]
π_2	0.271	[0.263, 0.286]
π_3	0.180	[0.177, 0.197]
π_4	0.090	[0.083, 0.097]
π_5	0.036	[0.031, 0.040]
π_6	0.012	[0.008, 0.013]
$E\{\alpha_1\}$	7.389	[7.232, 8.484]

4.3   A Markov Chain with a Random Time Clock

Suppose $\{X_n, n \geq 0\}$ is a Markov chain with states 0, 1, 2, 3, 4 and transition matrix

$$
P = \begin{bmatrix}
.2 & .3 & .2 & .1 & .2 \\
.2 & .2 & .3 & .2 & .1 \\
.1 & .2 & .2 & .3 & .2 \\
.2 & .1 & .2 & .2 & .3 \\
.3 & .2 & .1 & .2 & .2
\end{bmatrix} .
$$

Let $\{N(t), t \geq 0\}$ be a Poisson process with rate 1. Suppose the Markov chain and the Poisson process are probabilistically independent of one another. Now let

$$
X(t) = X_n \qquad \text{if} \qquad N(t) = n
$$

for $t \geq 0$ and n = 0, 1, 2, ... That is, the transitions of the Markov chain occur at the times given by the Poisson process. Then, the process $\{X(t), t \geq 0\}$ is a Markov process, and is often referred to as a Markov chain with a "random time clock" or a "Markov chain subordinated to a Poisson process." The importance of this particular kind of Markov process is due to its inherent simplicity and the fact that every Markov process in continuous time having a finite number of states and stationary transition probabilities can be represented as an appropriate Markov chain with a random time clock.

Since the matrix P has all positive components, the chain $\{X_n, n \geq 0\}$ has a steady-state distribution in the sense of (3.1). Moreover, $\{X(t), t \geq 0\}$ has a steady-state distribution in the sense of (3.8) and it is clear that the steady-state distributions of $\{X(t), t \geq 0\}$ and $\{X_n, n \geq 0\}$ are the same.

For the process $\{X(t), t \geq 0\}$, put $X(0) = 0 = X_0$ and $R_1 = 0$. For $k \geq 1$, let L_k denote the duration of the kth visit to state 0 , and R_{k+1} the first time t after time $R_k + L_k$ at which $X(t) = 0$. That is, R_k gives the kth entry time to the zero state. Then $\{R_k, k \geq 1\}$ is a sequence of regeneration times for $\{X(t), t > 0\}$. The choice of 0 as return state is arbitrary.

We now present results of a sample simulation run of this chain. The variable X has the steady-state distribution of $\{X(t), t \geq 0\}$, and $\pi_i = P\{X = i\}$ for $0 \leq i \leq 4$. As in Section 3, $\gamma_k = R_{k+1} - R_k$; also, $\hat{\gamma}_k$ denotes the number of changes of state in the process $\{X(t), t \geq 0\}$ over the time interval $[R_k, R_{k+1})$.

The simulation run consisted of 1,000 cycles of returns to state 0 , and approximate 95% confidence intervals were obtained for various parameters In each case the confidence interval surrounded the true value of the parameter being estimated.

TABLE 4.4 <u>Simulation Results for Markov Chain with a Random Time</u>
<u>Clock</u> (run length = 1,000 cycles, level of confidence = 95%)

Parameter	Theoretical Value	Confidence Interval
$E\{X\}$	2.000	[1.972, 2.040]
$E\{X^2\}$	6.000	[5.910, 6.191]
π_0	0.200	[0.194, 0.211]
π_1	0.200	[0.187, 0.205]
π_2	0.200	[0.191, 0.208]
π_3	0.200	[0.188, 0.205]
π_4	0.200	[0.197, 0.214]
$E\{\gamma_1\}$	6.250	[5.900, 6.427]
$E\{\hat{\gamma}_1\}$	5.000	[4.721, 5.143]

5.0   THE REGENERATIVE APPROACH AND DISCRETE-EVENT SIMULATIONS

In this section we discuss the relationship between regenerative simulations and general discrete-event simulations. We first discuss discrete-event simulations through a queueing example and then illustrate the application of the regenerative approach to more general discrete-event simulations.

5.1   Estimating Steady-State Queue-Length Using Event Times

Consider a discrete-event simulation of the queue-size process $\{Q(t), t \geq 0\}$ in a single-server queueing system. Suppose the interarrival times take the values 2, 4 and 6 each with probability 1/3, and the service times take the values 1 and 3 each with probability 1/2. The objective is to estimate $E\{Q\}$ where Q is the steady-state number of customers in the system.

Note that the simulation "regenerates itself" each time a customer arrives to find the server idle, as in the example of Section 2.1. We could therefore use such regeneration points to estimate $E\{Q\}$, applying the methods in Section 3. Note, however, that the existence of these regeneration points, as well as those in the earlier queueing example, follows from the special structure of queueing models. We shall now show that there are other regeneration points in this system which arise due to the structure of discrete-event simulations in general rather than the specific queueing structure.

The queue-size process is typically simulated by generating recursively two types of events: customer arrival events and service completion events.

At the time of a customer arrival event, the interarrival time to the next customer arrival (a random variable) is computed and the corresponding new customer arrival event is stored for future consideration. Also, if the server is idle, a service time (also a random variable) is computed for the customer just arrived and the corresponding service completion event is stored for future consideration. At the time of a service completion event, a new service time is generated for the next customer in line, if any, and a new service completion event stored for future consideration. Thus, the simulation consists of successive consideration of events, in the order of their occurrence, each event in turn generating possible new future events. Observe that $Q(t)$ can only change state at the event times and that interarrival and service times are generated only at event times.

Note that, at any given time t, the state of the simulation is completely specified by

1. the queue-size $Q(t)$,

2. the time duration $U(t)$ to the next customer arrival event, and

3. the time duration $V(t)$ to the next service completion event, if any.

That is, these three variables are the only quantities observed up to time t which have any effect on the future probabilistic evolution of the simulation after time t. This suggests a generalized state-vector for the simulation

$$\underset{\sim}{X}(t) = \begin{pmatrix} Q(t) \\ U(t) \\ V(t) \end{pmatrix} \, ,$$

which may be used in defining regeneration times for the simulation.

In order to illustrate these ideas more clearly, suppose that the simulation run results in the data given by Table 5.1. To illustrate the table, at time 0 the simulation begins by generating the arrival time of the first customer, which happens to be at time 6. There is thus only one future event at this time, a customer arrival at time 6. Now advancing the clock to time 6, $Q(t)$ is increased by one to reflect the customer arrival, and a new interarrival time is generated, which happens to be 2 (i.e., the next customer will arrive at time $6 + 2 = 8$). Also, a service time of 3 is generated for the first customer who has just arrived. There are now two future events: a new arrival 2 time units hence, and a service completion 3 time units hence. Since the earliest future event is an arrival at time $6 + 2 = 8$, the clock is now advanced to that time. At time 8 , $Q(t)$ is again increased by one, and the interarrival time for the third customer is generated. Note, however, that no service time is generated at this time since the server is still busy with the first customer. Now the simulation continues in this manner, with the clock advanced successively to the earliest future events and with new future events generated at each event time.

Now, observe that, in this example,

$$\underset{\sim}{X}(16) = \underset{\sim}{X}(32) = \begin{pmatrix} 1 \\ 4 \\ 3 \end{pmatrix} \quad ,$$

and that $\underset{\sim}{X}(9) = \underset{\sim}{X}(36)$ and $\underset{\sim}{X}(12) = \underset{\sim}{X}(24)$. Thus, for example, at the times 16 and 32 the number of people in the queue is the same, the times to future events are the same, and the specification of future events is the same.

TABLE 5.1 Simulation of Queueing System

Time t	Event	Interarrival Time Generated	Service Time Generated	Q(t)	Time U(t) to next Arrival Event	Time V(t) to next Service Completion Event
0	Start	6	-	0	6	-
6	Arrival	2	3	1	2	3
8	Arrival	2	-	2	2	1
9	Service Completion	-	3	1	1	3
10	Arrival	6	-	2	6	2
12	Service Completion	-	1	1	4	1
13	Service Completion	-	-	0	3	-
16	Arrival	4	3	1	4	3
19	Service Completion	-	-	0	1	-
20	Arrival	4	1	1	4	1
21	Service Completion	-	-	0	3	-
24	Arrival	4	1	1	4	1
25	Service Completion	-	-	0	3	-
28	Arrival	2	2	1	2	2
30	Arrival and Service Completion	2	1	1	2	1
31	Service Completion	-	-	0	2	0
32	Arrival	4	3	1	4	3
35	Service Completion	-	-	0	1	-
36	Arrival	1	3	1	1	3
37	Arrival	4	-	2	4	2
39	Service Completion	-	3	1	2	3
41	Arrival	2	-	2	2	1
42	Service Completion	-	1	1	1	1
43	Arrival and Service Completion	5	3	1	5	3

Hence, the simulation starts over with the same probabilistic behavior each time

it enters the "state" $\begin{pmatrix} 1 \\ 4 \\ 3 \end{pmatrix}$. Suppose now that the simulation is continued

beyond time 43, and let R_k be the kth time that $\underset{\sim}{X}(t) = \begin{pmatrix} 1 \\ 4 \\ 3 \end{pmatrix}$. We have

$R_1 = 16$ and $R_2 = 32$. Let $\gamma_k = R_{k+1} - R_k$ and

$$Z_k = \int_{R_k}^{R_{k+1}} Q(t)\,dt$$

for $k \geq 1$. Then, the times $\{R_k, k > 1\}$ are regeneration times for the
process $\{\underset{\sim}{X}(t), t \geq 0\}$ so that (Z_1, γ_1) , (Z_2, γ_2) , . . . are independent
and identically distributed and

$$E\{Q\} = E\{Z_1\}/E\{\gamma_1\} .$$

Note that, unlike the queueing example of Section 2.1, these results follow
from the nature of the discrete-event simulation (i.e., the use of event times)
and not from the special queueing structure. Thus, the regenerative approach
of Section 3 can be applied.

Suppose now that we consider the same example but that the interarrival
times are uniformly distributed over the interval $[1, 3]$ and the service times
are uniformly distributed over $[1, 2]$. Then the successive entry times of the

vector $\underset{\sim}{X}(t)$ to the state $\begin{pmatrix} 1 \\ 4 \\ 3 \end{pmatrix}$ are still regeneration times for the process by the same argument as above. Under these circumstances, however, the expected time between regeneration times is infinite, so that the regenerative technique cannot be applied directly. However, in Section 6 we shall consider approximation techniques which can be used with the regenerative approach in such a case.

Thus, we see there are expanded possibilities for applying the regenerative approach when we look at times to future events, and we now broaden these observations to general discrete-event simulations.

5.2   Application to Discrete-Event Simulations

We can think of a discrete-event simulation as a realization of two vector stochastic processes $\{\underset{\sim}{T}(t), t \geq 0\}$ and $\{\underset{\sim}{M}(t), t \geq 0\}$ that change state at a finite number (in finite time) of __event times__ $0 \leq t_1 \leq t_2 \leq t_3 \ldots$ generated in the course of the simulation. At time t_n , the vector $T_n = \underset{\sim}{T}(t_n)$ is a chronologically ordered listing of the times to all future events that have been generated through the completion of the nth event. Thus, the first component of $\underset{\sim}{T}_n$ gives the time duration between the nth and $(n + 1)$th events. Note, however, that the second component of $\underset{\sim}{T}_n$, if any, gives only a "tentative" time to the $(n + 2)$nd event, since an earlier event could possibly be generated at time t_{n+1} . The vector $\underset{\sim}{M}_n = \underset{\sim}{M}(t_n)$ consists of a number of variables describing the simulation model at time t_n , including any variables needed to specify which events are to occur at the times given by $\underset{\sim}{T}_n$. The simulation consists, therefore of generating a realization of

$$\underset{\sim}{X}(t) = \begin{pmatrix} \underset{\sim}{T}(t) \\ \underset{\sim}{M}(t) \end{pmatrix} \quad .$$

In practice, the processes $\underline{T}(t)$ and $\underline{M}(t)$ are generated as follows. At the start of the simulation, $\underline{T}(t)$ and $\underline{M}(t)$ are set to initial values $\underline{T}_0$ and $\underline{M}_0$, respectively, and the simulation clock is set to $t_0 = 0$. The time of the first event is obtained from the first component of $\underline{T}_0$, and the event type is specified by observing $\underline{M}_0$. The clock is then advanced to time t_1 , and the first event is executed. Event execution consists of generating the vectors $\underline{T}_1$ and $\underline{M}_1$ based upon observing $\underline{T}_0$, $\underline{M}_0$, and one or more random variables produced at time t_1 . The time of the second event is then obtained from $\underline{T}_1$ and the process is repeated recursively.

These ideas are easily illustrated by having a closer look at the (discrete-event) simulation of a single-server queue. Figure 5.2 shows how a simulation of a single-server queue would be modeled in the above framework. At any given time there are two possible events: a customer arrival or a service completion. The first component of $\underline{M}_n = (M_{n1}, M_{n2}, M_{n3})$ describes the first future event, and the second component describes the second future event, if any. These components may take on the values 0, 1, or 2 with 0 denoting no event, 1 denoting an arrival, and 2 denoting a service completion. The third component M_{n3} denotes the number of customers in the system. Interarrival-time and service-time random variables are denoted, respectively by u and v .

This leads to the notion of a stationary simulation. Let $\underline{X}_n = \begin{pmatrix} \underline{T}_n \\ \underline{M}_n \end{pmatrix}$. Given values for $\underline{T}_n$ and $\underline{M}_n$, we note that $\underline{T}_{n+1}$ and $\underline{M}_{n+1}$ are determined following the generation of one or more random variables. One can thus talk about state transition probabilities from $\underline{X}_n$ to $\underline{X}_{n+1}$.

79

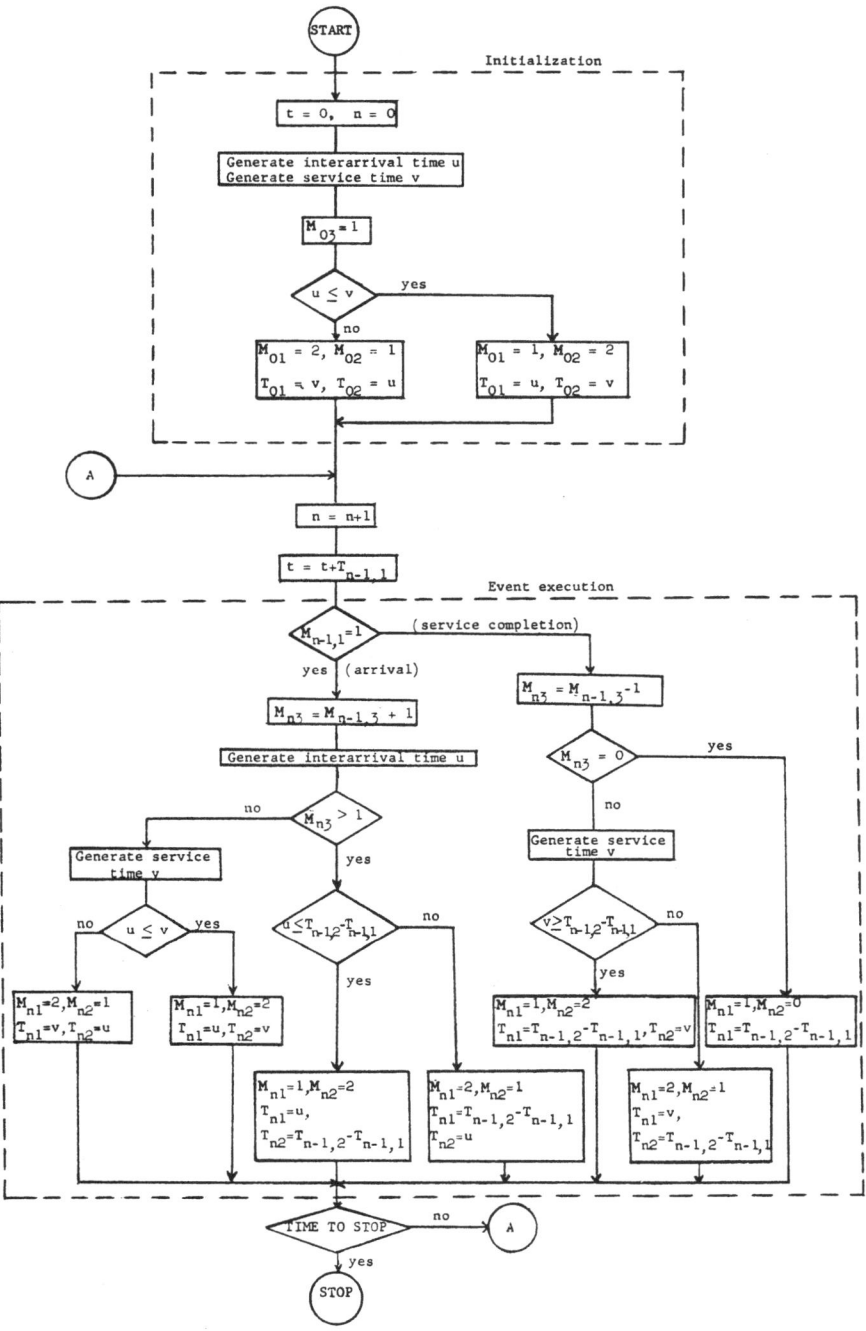

Figure 5.2 - Discrete-Event Simulation of a GI/G/1 Queue

The simulation is said to be stationary if these transition probabilities are independent of n . The queueing system simulation is stationary because the interarrival times and the service times both are sequences of independent and identically distributed random variables, i.e., they do not depend on the time of the simulation. Now, for a stationary simulation, each time $\underline{X}(t) = \underline{s}$, where $\underline{s}$ is some fixed simulation state-vector, the simulation "regenerates itself." That is, each $\underline{X}(t) = \underline{s}$, we know the state variables are the same, the times to future events are the same, the future event types are the same, and the probability distributions for random variables to be generated are the same. Therefore, the entry times to $\underline{s}$ are regeneration times for the stationary discrete-event simulation $\{\underline{X}(t), t \geq 0\}$. We can thus speak of cycles in the simulation as being time intervals on the simulation clock between successive returns to $\underline{s}$, and identical random variables defined in successive cycles are then independent and identically distributed. If $\underline{X}(t) \Longrightarrow \underline{X}$ as $t \to \infty$ and f is a "nice" real-valued function such that $E\{|f(\underline{X})|\} < \infty$, then we can estimate $E\{f(\underline{X})\}$ using the regenerative approach as follows. Let Z_j be the integral of $f[\underline{X}(t)]$ over the jth cycle and γ_j the length of the jth cycle. The pairs $\{(Z_j, \gamma_j), j \geq 1\}$ are independent and identically distributed. If $E\{\gamma_1\} < \infty$ then $E\{f(\underline{X})\} = E\{Z_1\}/E\{\gamma_1\}$, and the method of Section 3 may be used to obtain a confidence interval for $E\{f(\underline{X})\}$. If the expected time between returns to $\underline{s}$ is not finite, then the approximation techniques of Section 6 may be used.

We conclude this section by remarking that the clever simulator may not find it necessary to define a state space as rich as that discussed above

in applying the regenerative method to a specific simulation. In many simulations, simpler state-space descriptions are sufficient to guarantee a
regenerative process. One example is the inventory distribution model of
Section 4.1 where we have not found it necessary to include the times to
future events in the state space.

6.0   APPROXIMATION TECHNIQUES

This tutorial has been concerned with the problem of estimating a parameter which is associated with the steady-state distribution of a stochastic
process being simulated. A methodology for obtaining confidence intervals for
such parameters has been presented in Section 3. The crucial requirements for
applying this methodology are (i) that the process repeatedly return to some
fixed state (or region), (ii) that the expected time between returns be finite,
and (iii) that the process start afresh probabilistically each time it enters
the fixed state (or region).

While the regenerative method appears to be attractive when it can be
applied, there are many regenerative simulations of interest in which the
expected time between successive returns is not finite, as we have observed
in Section 5. Or, while the expected time between returns might be finite, it
may not be small enough so that a reasonable number of regeneration times may
be observed in the course of the simulation. Finally, there are many simulations which are not regenerative processes but for which modified regenerative
techniques may be applicable. In this section we discuss two approximation
techniques which appear promising in such circumstances. These techniques are
"approximate regeneration" and "partial state-space discretization." The ideas
involved are best illustrated through a specific example.

Suppose we are simulating a single-server queue having interarrival
times which are exponentially distributed with mean 20 and service times which
are exponentially distributed with mean 10, and that our goal is to estimate
$E\{W\}$, the expected steady-state waiting time. It is well known that the

successive waiting times may be computed by

$$W_{n+1} = \max\{0, W_n + v_n - u_n\} \qquad (6.1)$$

where u_n is the interarrival time between customers n and $n+1$ and v_n is the service time of customer n. Thus, in practice, the system would be simulated by recursively computing W_n as in (6.1). Now suppose we consider the successive returns to the state 10 by the sequence of customer waiting times $\{W_n, n \geq 1\}$. That is, if β_k is the kth value of n such that $W_n = 10$, then our attention will focus on the times $\{\beta_k, k \geq 1\}$. Then in view of (6.1), it is easy to see that the times $\{\beta_k, k \geq 1\}$ are regeneration times for the process $\{W_n, n \geq 1\}$, since each time $W_n = 10$, the succeeding waiting times given by (6.1) are generated in an identical fashion starting with this value. However, because the distributions of both the interarrival times and the service times are continuous, the expected time between returns to this regenerative state are not finite.[1] Thus, the method of Section 3 is not directly applicable for obtaining a confidence interval for $E\{W\}$ using the regeneration times $\{\beta_k, k \geq 1\}$. We therefore look to approximation techniques for circumventing this difficulty, and such techniques are presented in Sections 6.1 and 6.2.

---

[1] Note that the returns to any fixed waiting time are regeneration times for the simulation but only the returns to the zero state, as considered in Section 2.1, are such that the expected cycle length is finite.

6.1   Approximate Regeneration

Suppose we let $\beta_k(\epsilon)$ denote the kth time the process $\{W_n, n \geq 1\}$ enters the "trapping" interval $[10 - \epsilon, 10 + \epsilon]$, where $\epsilon > 0$ is fixed. Then, the expected time between entries to the trapping interval is finite and decreases as ϵ is increased. Note, however, that the times $\beta_k(\epsilon)$ are not regeneration times for the process $\{W_n, n \geq 1\}$, since the waiting times of customers numbered $\beta_k(\epsilon)$ can fall anywhere in the interval $[10 - \epsilon, 10 + \epsilon]$. Thus, partitioning the output according to the times $\beta_k(\epsilon)$ does not result in independent identically distributed blocks. Nonethe-less, if ϵ is small, this situation ought to hold approximately, in the sense that random variables observed in successive blocks should have small correlation and should have nearly identical distributions. We are thus led to consider a statistical technique which treats the times $\beta_k(\epsilon)$ as though they are regeneration times. The simulation of the queue could then be analyzed by using the approach of Section 3, although the confidence intervals thereby obtained are only approximate.

Table 6.1 shows numerical results for the approximate regeneration tech-nique as applied to the above queueing example. For purposes of comparison, results are also shown using returns to the state $W_n = 0$ as true regeneration times. Observe that the length of the (approximate) regeneration cycle increases as the size of the trapping interval is made smaller. The length of the 80% confidence intervals on $E\{W\}$ do not differ significantly from those obtained by exact regeneration methods. Finally, accuracy is found to be best when the trapping interval is 6 ; worse when the length is 1 or 2 . This

TABLE 6.1 The Effect of Approximate Regeneration on Regeneration
Methodology (Based on 400 simulation replications of
1000 customers, each resulting in an 80% confidence
interval of E{W})

Trapping Interval (Trapping Interval Center is 10)	On expected length of regeneration cycle	90% Confidence Interval On expected length of 80% Confidence Interval for E{W}	On probability that 80% Confidence Interval for E{W} surrounds the true value E{W} = 10.0
[7, 13]	11.02 ± 0.08	3.96 ± 0.13	0.76 ± 0.04
[9, 11]	34.95 ± 0.55	4.07 ± 0.14	0.72 ± 0.04
[9.5, 10.5]	68.42 ± 3.15	3.81 ± 0.14	0.72 ± 0.04
Exact Regeneration (Regeneration Point is $W_n = 0$)	2.00 ± 0.01	4.01 ± 0.13	0.78 ± 0.03

somewhat surprising result may best be explained when one considers the correlations observed between successive cycles in each case. In separate runs of
100,000 customers, correlations were estimated for the sum of customer waiting
times in successive cycles. These correlations were found to be 0.01, - 0.01 ,
and -0.01 , respectively, when the trapping interval lengths were 6, 2 and 1.
In other words, the assumption of approximate regeneration would appear to be
a very good one in each case. The decrease in accuracy which occurs with the
decrease in trapping interval length may then be explained by the decrease in the
number of cycles, so that the large-sample approximations of Section 3 are less

appropriate. The reader is cautioned, however, that this will not always be the case when using this method, as smaller trapping intervals will often be required to improve the approximate regenerative assumption. In this particular case, the assumption was found to be good for each trapping interval, so that the number of cycles became the more critical issue.

The preceding example suggests the following "approximate regeneration technique" for those simulations having a "return state" $\underset{\sim}{X}_0$ for which the expected time between returns to $\underset{\sim}{X}_0$ is not finite:

1. Choose a "small" region A surrounding $\underset{\sim}{X}_0$ such that the expected time between returns to A is finite and is small enough so that several returns would be observed in the course of the simulation.

2. Assume that the simulation approximately "starts over" each time it returns to A .

3. Redefine the variables β_j, α_j, and Y_j (of Section 3), in terms of returns to A rather than returns to $\underset{\sim}{X}_0$. (In the con-continuous-time case, the variables R_j, γ_j, and Z_j would be redefined.)

4. Compute confidence intervals as though (Y_1, α_1) , (Y_2, α_2) , . . . are independent and identically distributed and as though

$$E\{f(\underset{\sim}{X})\} = E\{Y_1\}/E\{\alpha_1\} \quad .$$

Note that such a method could be applied to the general discrete-event simulations discussed in Section 5. To illustrate, recall the queueing example of that section in which an expanded state vector for the simulation was given by

$$\underset{\sim}{X}(t) = \begin{pmatrix} Q(t) \\ U(t) \\ V(t) \end{pmatrix} \quad ,$$

where $Q(t)$ is the number of customers in the system at time t , $U(t)$ is the time duration to the next customer arrival event after t , and $V(t)$ is the time duration to the next service completion event, if any, after t . Recall that each time the process returns to a state $\underset{\sim}{X}_0$, the simulation regenerates itself, but that if the interarrival and service time distributions are continuous, then the expected time between regenerations is not finite. Thus, the method of approximate regeneration would appear to be applicable here. More specifically, we could select a region A , say, as

$$A = \{Q(t) = 1 \ , \ 2 \le U(t) \le 4 \ , \ 2 \le V(t) \le 3\} \ ,$$

assume that the process is "regenerated approximately" each time it returns to A , and apply the methods of Section 3 as though they were true regeneration points. Alternatively, we might be more liberal and select A as

$$A = \{Q(t) = 1\} \ ;$$

that is, we say that the process $\underset{\sim}{X}(t)$ is approximately regenerated each time that $Q(t) = 1$, regardless of the values for $U(t)$ and $V(t)$. Such a choice would be more easily programmed and would also result in more frequent "regenerations."

Note, there is no definite answer to the question of how liberal the choice of the trapping region A may be while still maintaining a good approximation. Limited empirical experience with this technique suggests that the approximations are good with quite liberal selection of such regions. However, the experience to this date is minimal, and further research is definitely needed to help answer this question.

6.2 Partial State-Space Discretization

Returning to the example of the customer waiting times $\{W_n, n \geq 1\}$, suppose we consider a modified waiting time process $\{W_n', n \geq 1\}$ which differs from the original process $\{W_n, n \geq 1\}$ as follows. For each customer whose waiting time falls in a trapping interval $[10 - \epsilon, 10 + \epsilon]$, the waiting time is set to equal to 10, and the succeeding waiting times given by (6.1) are also based on this modified value. This amounts to a discretization of the state space in the neighborhood of 10.

Now the entry times $\{\beta_k'(\epsilon), k \geq 1\}$ to 10 in the modified process are regeneration times for the modified process. Furthermore, since $\epsilon > 0$, the expected time between successive regenerations in the modified process is finite. We may thus apply the regenerative method to analyze statistically the modified process, as an approximation of the original process. The approximation should improve as ϵ is made smaller. At the same time, however, the

expected time between regeneration times increases as ϵ decreases, with
potential impact on the validity of the large-sample assumptions needed for
the regenerative method.

Table 6.2 shows numerical results for this approximation technique
based on 400 replications of the confidence intervals so obtained. We see,
as expected,

Table 6.2 The Effect of Partial State-Space Discretization on
Regeneration Methodology (Based on 400 simulation
replications of 1000 customers, each resulting in an
80% confidence interval for $E\{W'\}$)

Trapping Interval (Regeneration Point is $W_n' = 10$)	90% Confidence Interval	
	On expected length of regeneration cycle.	On expected length of 80% Confidence Interval for $E\{W'\}$
[7, 13]	11.12 ± 0.10	3.88 ± 0.13
[9, 11]	34.27 ± 0.56	3.94 ± 0.13
[9.5, 10.5]	69.70 ± 1.66	4.11 ± 0.19
Nondiscrete Model (Regeneration Point is $W_n = 0$)	2.00 ± 0.01	4.01 ± 0.13

that the length of the regeneration cycle increases as the trapping interval is
made smaller (i.e., discretization about $W_n' = 10$ is made less severe). Thus,

with a small trapping interval, one must be careful that the number of regeneration cycles is not so small as to render the large-sample approximations inappropriate. We see also in Table 6.2 that the lengths of the confidence intervals obtained for $E\{W'\}$ are about the same as those obtained for $E\{W\}$ in the original nondiscrete model.

Note, in Table 6.2, we have <u>not</u> estimated the probability of the confidence interval surrounding the expected steady-state waiting time in the original process. To do so would not be meaningful since, in fact, such confidence intervals are for the modified process, not the original process. The key question, of course, is the extent to which the parameter from the modified process differs from the true parameter of interest.

The preceding example suggests the following "<u>partial state-space-discretization technique</u>" for those simulations having a "return state" $\underset{\sim}{X}_0$ for which the expected time between returns is not finite:

1. Choose a "small" region A surrounding the "return state" $\underset{\sim}{X}_0$. Define a modified process, say $\{\underset{\sim}{X}'_n , n \geq 1\}$, such that when $\underset{\sim}{X}'_n \in A$, we set $\underset{\sim}{X}'_n = \underset{\sim}{X}_0$. Note this calls for modification of the simulation.

2. The modified process is a regenerative process with finite expected cycle length.

3. Apply the regenerative method to estimate the appropriate steady-state parameter(s) of the modified process, as an approximation of the original process.

6.3   Concluding Remarks

There are two advantages of the approximate regeneration technique when compared to the partial state-space discretization technique. First, there is no distortion in the state space, as the original process is analyzed directly. Second, the programming is simpler, being no more difficult than the exact regeneration technique. This is particularly important when considering application to potentially complex discrete-event simulations which are formulated as in Section 5. The principal disadvantage of approximate regeneration is that the simulator does not know how good the approximate regenerative assumption is and thus the accuracy of the confidence interval. This disadvantage can be offset somewhat by measuring the correlation between successive cycles. If the correlation is low and the sample size (number of cycles) is sufficiently large, then the accuracy of the confidence interval should be close to that claimed in the statement of confidence.

Thus, the technique of approximate regeneration produces a possibly inaccurate, non-rigorous confidence interval on the original process, while partial state-space discretization produces rigorous confidence intervals on a distorted process, which may in addition be difficult to program. At this point, the simulator must make a subjective judgment on which method to use.

7.0   ALTERNATIVE RATIO ESTIMATORS

As we have seen, the regenerative method for estimating steady-state parameters via simulation requires the simulator to estimate the ratio of two means. One method for obtaining a confidence interval for the ratio of two means was given in Section 3. In this section we examine the problem of ratio estimation more closely and consider several alternative point estimates and confidence intervals for ratios which can be used in conjunction with the regenerative method.

Suppose we are given the observations (Y_1, α_1) , $(Y_2, \alpha_2) \ldots$, (Y_n, α_n) which are independent and identically distributed, and the problem is to estimate $r \equiv E\{Y_1\}/E\{\alpha_1\}$.

As in Section 3, let $\bar{Y} = \frac{1}{n}\sum_{i=1}^{n} Y_i$, $\bar{\alpha} = \frac{1}{n}\sum_{i=1}^{n} \alpha_i$,

$$s_{11} = \frac{1}{n-1}\sum_{i=1}^{n}(Y_i - \bar{Y})^2 \ , \qquad s_{22} = \frac{1}{n-1}\sum_{i=1}^{n}(\alpha_i - \bar{\alpha})^2 \ , \quad \text{and}$$

$$s_{12} = \frac{1}{n-1}\sum_{i=1}^{n}(Y_i - \bar{Y})(\alpha_i - \bar{\alpha}) \ . \quad \text{Suppose we are interested in a } 100(1 - \delta)\%$$

confidence interval for r .

We consider first the following point estimates for the ratio r :

Beale estimator

$$\hat{r}_b(n) = \frac{\bar{Y}}{\bar{\alpha}} \cdot \frac{(1 + s_{12}/n\bar{Y}\bar{\alpha})}{(1 + s_{22}/n\bar{\alpha}^2)} \quad ; \qquad (7.1)$$

Classical estimator

$$\hat{r}_c(n) \; = \; \frac{\overline{Y}}{\overline{\alpha}} \quad ; \tag{7.2}$$

Fieller estimator

$$\hat{r}_f(n) \; = \; \frac{\overline{Y}\,\overline{\alpha} - k_\delta\, s_{12}}{\overline{\alpha}^{\,2} - k_\delta s_{22}} \tag{7.3}$$

where $\; k_\delta = \left[\phi^{-1}\left(1 - \frac{\delta}{2}\right)\right]^2 \Big/ n \; ;$

Jackknife estimator

$$\hat{r}_j(n) \; = \; \frac{1}{n} \sum_{i=1}^{n} \theta_i \tag{7.4}$$

where $\; \theta_i = n(\overline{Y}/\overline{\alpha}) - (n-1)\left(\sum_{k \neq i} Y_k \Big/ \sum_{k \neq i} \alpha_k \right) \; ;$ and the

Tin Estimator

$$\hat{r}_t(n) \; = \; \frac{\overline{Y}}{\overline{\alpha}} \left[1 + \frac{1}{n}\left(\frac{s_{12}}{\overline{Y}\,\overline{\alpha}} - \frac{s_{22}}{\overline{\alpha}^2} \right) \right] \; . \tag{7.5}$$

The classical estimator was introduced as $\hat{r}$ in Section 3.3. All of these estimators are "strongly" consistent (converge to r with probability one as $n \to \infty$) and generally are biased. The Beale, jacknife, and Tin estimators were all developed in an effort to reduce the bias of the classical estimator.

The problem of constructing confidence intervals for r can be approached in a number of ways. As in Section 3.3, let $V_i = Y_i - r\alpha_i$. The V_i's are independent and identically distributed, and $E\{V_i\} = 0$. Putting $\sigma = E\{V_i^2\}$ and assuming $0 < \sigma < \infty$, we know by the central limit theorem that

$$\frac{\sum_{i=1}^{n} V_i}{\sigma n^{1/2}} \Longrightarrow N(0,1) \quad \text{as} \quad n \to \infty \; , \tag{7.6}$$

where $N(0,1)$ represents a normal random variable with mean zero and variance one, and the double arrow denotes convergence in distribution. Rewriting (7.6) we see that

$$\frac{n^{1/2} \left[\hat{r}_c(n) - r \right]}{(\sigma/\bar{\alpha})} \Longrightarrow N(0,1) \quad \text{as} \quad n \to \infty \; . \tag{7.7}$$

Note that (7.6) is simply a re-statement of (3.11), and (7.7) a restatement of (3.12). Since $n^{1/2} \left[\hat{r}_c(n) - \hat{r}_b(n) \right] \to 0$ and $n^{1/2} \left[\hat{r}_c(n) - \hat{r}_t(n) \right] \to 0$ as

$n \to \infty$ with probability one, we can replace $\hat{r}_c(n)$ in (7.7) by either $\hat{r}_b(n)$ or $\hat{r}_t(n)$ without changing the result. However, all of these statements about convergence to a $N(0, 1)$ random variable involve the constant σ. In most simulations the constant σ cannot be computed. For those cases where it has been computed the calculation is quite difficult. Thus, the crucial step in obtaining confidence intervals for r is to estimate the value of σ. The classical method for obtaining confidence intervals, which was given in Section 3.3, replaces σ in (7.7) by $\left[s_{11} - 2 \hat{r}_c s_{12} + \hat{r}_c^2 s_{22} \right]^{1/2} \equiv \hat{s}_c(n)$, and this yields the approximate $100(1 - \delta)\%$ confidence interval for r given by

$$
\hat{I}_c(n) = \left[\hat{r}_c - \frac{z_\delta^* \hat{s}_c}{\bar{\alpha} \, n^{1/2}} \quad , \quad \hat{r}_c + \frac{z_\delta^* \hat{s}_c}{\bar{\alpha} \, n^{1/2}} \right] \tag{7.8}
$$

where $z_\delta^* = \Phi^{-1}\left(1 - \frac{\delta}{2} \right)$. Note that (7.8) is identical to (3.14). Now, since either the Beale estimator $\hat{r}_b(n)$ or the Tin estimator $\hat{r}_t(n)$ can be substituted for $\hat{r}_c(n)$ in (7.7), we immediately have the following two variations of the confidence interval $\hat{I}_c(n)$:

$$
\hat{I}_{bc}(n) = \left[\hat{r}_b - \frac{z_\delta^* \hat{s}_c}{\bar{\alpha} \, n^{1/2}} \quad , \quad \hat{r}_b + \frac{z_\delta^* \hat{s}_c}{\bar{\alpha} \, n^{1/2}} \right] \tag{7.9}
$$

and

$$
\hat{I}_{tc}(n) = \left[\hat{r}_t - \frac{z_\delta^* \hat{s}_c}{\bar{\alpha} \, n^{1/2}} \quad , \quad \hat{r}_t + \frac{z_\delta^* \hat{s}_c}{\bar{\alpha} \, n^{1/2}} \right] . \tag{7.10}
$$

The Fieller method replaces σ in (7.7) by $\left[s_{11} - 2\,r\,s_{12} + r^2 s_{22}\right]^{1/2} \equiv \hat{s}_f(n)$,

so that (7.7) may be rewritten

$$\frac{\bar{\alpha}\,n^{1/2}\left[\bar{Y}/\bar{\alpha} - r\right]}{\left[s_{11} - 2\,r\,s_{12} + r^2 s_{22}\right]^{1/2}} \Longrightarrow N(0,1) \quad \text{as} \quad n \to \infty \quad .$$

Algebraic manipulation then leads to the following approximate $100(1 - \delta)\%$ confidence interval for r :

$$\hat{I}_f(n) = \left[\hat{r}_f - \frac{D^{1/2}}{(\bar{\alpha}^2 - k_\delta s_{22})} \;,\; \hat{r}_f + \frac{D^{1/2}}{(\bar{\alpha}^2 - k_\delta s_{22})}\right] \tag{7.11}$$

where $D = \left[\bar{Y}\,\bar{\alpha} - k_\delta\,s_{12}\right]^2 - \left[\bar{\alpha}^2 - k_\delta\,s_{22}\right]\cdot\left[\bar{Y}^2 - k_\delta\,s_{11}\right]$ and

$k_\delta = \left[\phi^{-1}\left(1 - \tfrac{\delta}{2}\right)\right]^2 \Big/ n$.

The final type of confidence interval considered here arises from the jackknife method. In terms of the notation introduced above, let

$$\hat{s}_j(n) = \left\{\sum_{i=1}^{n}\left[\theta_i - \hat{r}_j(n)\right]^2 \Big/ (n - 1)\right\}^{1/2} .$$

Then the following limit result provides a basis for a confidence interval:

$$\frac{\hat{r}_j(n) - r}{n^{1/2} \cdot \hat{s}_j(n)} \Longrightarrow N(0, 1) \quad \text{as} \quad n \to \infty \quad .$$

The jackknife method then yields the approximate $100(1 - \delta)\%$ confidence interval

$$\hat{I}_j(n) = \left[\hat{r}_j - \frac{z_\delta^* \hat{s}_j}{n^{1/2}} , \hat{r}_j + \frac{z_\delta^* \hat{s}_j}{n^{1/2}} \right] \quad . \tag{7.12}$$

In an effort to provide some guidance for simulators, the performance of these estimators was evaluated for versions of the stochastic models discussed in Section 2; namely, a single-server queue, an inventory model, and a repairman model. Both the small and large sample properties of the point and interval estimators described above were compared. A number of observations emerged from these experimental results and we give a brief summary of the conclusions drawn from the evaluation effort.

For short runs the jackknife method produced less biased point estimates and more accurate confidence intervals for r . Thus, the jackknife method is particularly appropriate for any short exploratory runs the simulator might make. The jackknife method does call, however, for a large memory requirement and for slightly more complex programming. Additional storage addresses of the order of 2n are required, where n is the number of cycles observed. (The entire sequence of Y_i's and α_i's must be saved to perform the final calculations.)

98

Should storage requirements for the jackknife method be excessive, then the Beale or Tin methods are recommended for point estimates and the classical method is recommended for interval estimates. The classical method for both point and interval estimates is the easiest to program, thereby making it an attractive candidate for long runs (since all these methods give equivalent results for long runs). The Fieller method for point and interval estimates is not recommended; it is found to be badly biased for small runs and more complicated than the classical method.

8.0   SOME OTHER RESULTS

In this section we indicate some other results which have been developed
in conjunction with the regenerative method for simulation analysis. All of
these results are of practical interest to simulators. The results include a
methodology to compare the performance of several systems which are being
simulated, a methodology for estimating quantiles of steady-state distributions,
a technique for gauging the sensitivity of statistical inferences relative to
changes in the input parameters for the simulation experiment, discrete-time
methods for continuous-time problems which can produce considerable savings in
computing time as well as increased statistical efficiency, investigations into
the determination of run length in simulations of stable stochastic systems, and
methods of reducing the variance of estimators of steady-state parameters in
regenerative simulations.

In this section we shall mention only briefly these various results so
that the reader may be aware of their existence. For more detail, the reader
should refer to the appropriate references given in Section 9.

8.1   Selecting the Best System

We indicate here a methodology which can be used in conjunction
with the regenerative method to compare the performance of several systems
which are being simulated. A good example of this is where several alternative system designs are being tested via simulation.

For the sake of discussion let us assume there are $k(\geq 2)$ alternative
system designs and that associated with each of the designs is a regenerative
process $\{X^i(t), t \geq 0\}$, $i = 1, 2, \ldots, k$, which will be simulated.
Further, suppose the measure of performance for the ith system is $r_i = E\{f(X^i)\}$,

the mean value of some given function f of the "steady-state" random variable X^i of the process $\{X^i(t), t \geq 0\}$. In particular, if the system being simulated is a repairman model, system performance might be based on the expected number of units operating. Then, in this case, our goal is to select from the k systems the one with the largest value of r_i , based on simulation experiments. (On the other hand, one can easily find examples where the goal would be to choose the system with the smallest value of r_i .)

To give some idea of the results which have been developed for comparing alternative systems, let us first consider the case where k = 2 . In this instance suppose we wish to compare r_1 and r_2 Suppose that system 1 is presently in operation, that system 2 is a proposed improvement, and we wish to test whether $r_1 = r_2$ or $r_1 < r_2$. Then, tests of hypotheses (which are of fixed level α) have been developed for making such comparisons.

For the general case of $k \geq 2$, suppose our interest lies in selecting the system with the largest r_i . In order to achieve this, suppose we decide on the following selection scheme. We begin by specifying two positive numbers P^* and δ^* . Our goal is then to select with probability P^* the system with the largest r_i , whenever that value of r_i is separated by at least δ^* from the other r_j's . There is, unfortunately, no fixed sample size procedure that will guarantee the above goal. This is due to the fact that certain variances are unknown and have to be estimated. However, two procedures have been developed for this problem. The first procedure is sequential and the second two-stage. The sequential procedure employs a stopping rule which is based on estimates of certain variances. The two-stage procedure uses the first stage to estimate these variances, with the length of the second stage then determined by the variance estimates.

8.2 Quantile Estimation

Instead of estimating $E\{f(\underline{X})\}$ the simulator might be interested in the quantiles of the distribution function of $f(\underline{X})$. To simplify this discussion we shall assume X is a real-valued random variable and take $f(x) = x$. Then, the problem is to estimate the quantiles of the distribution function F of X . The pth quantile $Q(p)$ of F is defined to be the lowest value of x such that $F(x) \geq p$, for $0 < p < 1$. For example, the .5 quantile is the median of the distribution for X , while the .75 quantile is that value x such that $P\{X \leq x\} = .75$ but $P\{X \leq y\} < .75$ for $y < x$. In the nice case, i.e., when the distribution function F is continuous, we have $Q(p) = F^{-1}(p)$. Estimating quantiles is a much more difficult problem than estimating moments.

From a practical standpoint quantile estimation is quite important. In designing the waiting room for a complex queueing system the characteristic of interest may be the .90 quantile of the distribution of the steady-state number of customers waiting, i.e., that number of waiting places which will be sufficient 90% of the time. Similarly, in designing a repair system, such as described in Section 2.3, one may want to know the .95 quantile of the distribution of the number of units at the repair facility in order to decide how many spare units are adequate.

Methods of quantile estimation have been developed in the context of regenerative simulations. For details of these methods, the reader is directed to the references given in Section 9.

8.3   Sensitivity Analysis: A Polynomial Approximation Technique

Using the regenerative method, the simulator can obtain a con-
fidence interval for the quantity $E\{f(\underline{X})\}$ for any particular choice of the
simulation input parameters. Suppose, however, that some input parameter λ
is not known with certainty, but rather that its value lies in the interval
$[a, b]$. For example, in the repairman model of Section 2, the simulator may
know only that the failure rate for operating units lies somewhere in the
interval $[3, 6]$, rather than knowing that its exact value is 5. Thus,
letting $g(\lambda) = E\{f(\underline{X})|\lambda\}$, it would be helpful to have a technique for com-
puting a confidence band for the function g over the interval $[a, b]$, as
well as a confidence interval for $g(\lambda)$ for each $a \leq \lambda \leq b$, without
requiring the simulation of every possible value of λ in this interval.

In those cases where g is a polynomial of degree K , a technique
has been developed for computing confidence bands and confidence intervals
over $[a, b]$. The technique requires the simulator to select $K + 1$
distinct values of λ in the interval $[a, b]$, say $a \leq \lambda_1 < \lambda_2 < \cdots$
$< \lambda_K < \lambda_{K+1} \leq b$, and then to perform $K + 1$ independent simulation runs,
where the jth run results in a confidence interval for $g(\lambda_i)$, $i = 1 , \ldots ,$
$K + 1$.

While $g(\lambda) = E\{f(\underline{X})|\lambda\}$ may not be an exact polnomial in λ , it
can be approximated by a polynomial function, the level of accuracy in the
approximation increasing as the degree of the approximating polynomial function
increases. Thus, the above technique for computing confidence bands and confidence intervals for polynomial functions is indeed useful.

8.4   Discrete Time Methods for Continuous Time Processes

Suppose that the simulation process of interest is a continuous time Markov chain $\{X(t), t \geq 0\}$. If this simulation is implemented in a straightforward manner, it is necessary to generate exponentially distributed holding times in the various states in order to determine the times between state transitions. In this section, we indicate a simple procedure which avoids these time-consuming computations and which also improves the accuracy of the estimates obtained by the regenerative approach.

Let m_i denote the mean holding time in state i . The important fact is that the steady-state distribution of $\{X(t), t \geq 0\}$ depends on the distribution of the holding times in the various states only through their means. Hence, if the process $\{X(t), t \geq 0\}$ is modified by letting the holding times in state i be constant with value m_i , then the modified process will have the same stationary distribution as $\{X(t), t \geq 0\}$, and hence the same value of $r = E\{f(X)\}$. But the modified process does not require the generation of exponential holding times, and so the computational savings can be quite significant. Furthermore, it can be shown that the value of $\sigma / E\{\alpha_1\}$ for the modified process is less than that for the original process. Recalling that $\sigma / E\{\alpha_1\}$ is the parameter which appears in the denominator of the central limit theorem for r , we see that the modified process will also lead to shorter confidence intervals for r for a fixed number of cycles.

8.5   Stopping Rules for Regenerative Simulations

A situation frequently encountered by simulation practitioners is the requirement to carry out enough replications of a simulation (or to generate sufficient cycles in the regenerative approach) to obtain an estimate

of a given parameter which is judged to be "accurate enough" by the end user.
Recall from Section 3 that confidence intervals obtained by the regenerative
approach have a random width with an expected value which, for large samples,
is inversely proportional to the square root of the number of regeneration
cycles. Thus, one method of obtaining confidence intervals which are "accurate
enough" is to first obtain a confidence interval in a small "pilot" run and
then to estimate the size of confidence intervals to be obtained in more lengthy
runs, using the above proportionality factor. Note, however, that such a method
does not guarantee a confidence interval of the specified size, since the confidence interval width is still random (for a fixed length run or a fixed number
of cycles) and is not known until the run is completed.

Suppose that the aim of the simulator is in fact to run the simulation
until a confidence interval of predetermined size is obtained. Since the
length of the confidence interval obtained during a fixed-length simulation
will in general be random, the required simulation run length to obtain a fixed
length confidence interval will also be random. The specific termination
criterion used in the simulation is thus called a "random stopping rule."
Such stopping rules have been studied in some detail for the classical problem of estimating the mean and variance of a sequence of independent and
identically distributed random variables. None of this previous work, however,
is general enough to be applied to estimates which arise in stochastic simulations. Furthermore, this work is limited to so-called "fixed-width" confidence intervals, i.e., one must specify in advance the absolute width of the
interval desired when the simulation terminates. A more practical approach,
however, is to allow the width of the final interval to depend on the parameter

itself in some way, e.g., to specify that the interval will be at most 10% of the final point estimate at termination. We call this a "relative width" stopping criterion.

Recent work (motivated by the regenerative method) has extended the previous results, both as to the type of confidence interval which may be used, as well as to a very broad class of relative width criteria. One conclusion to be drawn from this recent work is that extreme caution should be exercised in applying such random stopping rules, as the accuracy of these methods may be very poor in cases where the simulation is stopped after a small number of observations; in this regard, pilot runs can be helpful in assessing the reasonableness of the stopping rules. Also, if the simulator only needs a rough, but valid, estimate of a given parameter, i.e., if a valid confidence interval having an unspecified and possibly large relative width is adequate, then a fixed stopping rule may be satisfactory. On the other hand, if a precise valid estimate of a given parameter is desired, i.e., a valid confidence interval having a specified small relative width, then a sequential stopping rule seems appropriate.

8.6   Variance Reduction for Regenerative Simulations

In this tutorial we have presented a methodology, based on regenerative processes, for obtaining point estimates and confidence intervals for steady-state parameters. In particular, if the parameter of interest is $r = E\{f(\underset{\sim}{X})\}$, then the regenerative approach, as based upon the results (3.3) and (3.4), suggests using the ratio $r_c(n) \equiv \bar{Y}/\bar{\alpha}$ as an estimate for the value of r in a simulation run consisting of n regenerative cycles. This then raises the important question of how to apply variance reduction techniques with the ratio estimator $\hat{r}_c(n)$. In most practical situations, one would

106

certainly like to have the minimum possible variance in the estimation for a given amount of computing time (e.g., number of cycles allowed).

The problem of variance reduction in regenerative simulations has been explored very recently in the context of queueing systems, primarily the single-server queue, and in the context of Markov processes. Details of this work can be found in the references provided in Section 9.

9.0   BIBLIOGRAPHIC NOTE

We now give a brief survey of the relevant literature on the regenerative approach for stochastic simulations. We do so by relating the various references to Sections 1 through 8 of this tutorial presentation.

<u>Section</u>   Previous survey reports on the regenerative method are [15] and [16]. Both of these are helpful in furthering one's understanding of the method, and both contain extensive lists of references dealing with the regenerative method. Also helpful is the report [23] which provides detailed discussions on application of the regenerative method to a variety of models. A succinct introduction to statistical problems in simulation is given in Chapter 15 of [11]. The forthcoming monograph [18] will provide a rigorous development of the regenerative approach, and the various results, for simulation analysis.

<u>Section 2</u> The regenerative method as described in this tutorial presentation was set forth for queueing systems in [4], and then for Markov chains in [5]. The generalization to regenerative processes was given in [6]. Historically, it was suggested in [2] that simulations of queueing systems with Poisson arrivals could be analyzed by using their regenerative structure. The idea was partially developed in [20]. More recently, in work concurrent with [4] and [5], application of the regenerative idea to multi-server queues can be found in [8] and [9].

<u>Section 3</u> The source for this section is [6], which also discusses, and provides further references on, the subject of regenerative stochastic processes. An introduction to regenerative processes is also given in [1].

Section 4 The inventory example is from [6]. The particles-in-a-box Markov chain and the Markov chain with a random time clock are discussed from a simulation standpoint in [23].

Section 5 This section is motivated by the discussion of discrete-event simulations in [6].

Section 6 The motivation for this section is [7], where four approximation techniques, including approximate regeneration and partial state-space discretization, are discussed and compared in a queueing context.

Section 7 This section is based on [13] which provides numerical results for the evaluation of the various ratio estimators and confidence intervals.

Section 8 The methodology for comparing the performance of several systems which are being simulated is given in [14]. The sample quantile approach for estimating quantiles is presented in [17]; an alternate approach is proposed in [25]. The approximation technique for a general polynomial function is given in [3], the linear case was treated earlier in [4], and the quadratic case in [5]. Discrete time methods for continuous time processes are treated at length in [12]; short summaries are provided in [15] and [23]. Various stopping rules for determining run length are explored in [22] and [24]. Variance reduction techniques are discussed in [19] and [21] for simulations of queueing systems and in [10] for simulations of Markov processes; further work is in progress on the problem of variance reduction for regenerative simulations.

109

REFERENCES

[1] ÇINLAR, E. (1975). *Introduction to Stochastic Processes*. Prentice-Hall, Englewood Cliffs, N. J.

[2] COX, D. R. and SMITH, W. L. (1961). *Queues*. Methuen, London.

[3] CRANE, M. A. (1975). Techniques of Response Surface Estimation, with Applications in Computer Simulation. Technical Report No. 86-19, Control Analysis Corporation, Palo Alto, California.

[4] CRANE, M. A. and IGLEHART, D. L. (1974). Simulating Stable Stochastic Systems, I: General Multi-Server Queues. *J. Assoc. Comput. Mach*. 21, 103-113.

[5] CRANE, M. A. and IGLEHART, D. L. (1974). Simulating Stable Stochastic Systems, II: Markov Chains. *J. Assoc. Comput. Mach*. 21, 114-123.

[6] CRANE, M. A. and IGLEHART, D. L. (1975). Simulating Stable Stochastic Systems, III: Regenerative Processes and Discrete-Event Simulations. *Operations Res*. 23, 33-45.

[7] CRANE, M. A. and IGLEHART, D. L. (1975). Simulating Stable Stochastic Systems, IV: Approximation Techniques. *Management Sci*. 21, 1215-1224.

[8] FISHMAN, G. S. (1973). Statistical Analysis for Queueing Simulations. *Management Sci*. 20, 363-369.

[9] FISHMAN, G. S. (1974). Estimation in Multiserver Queueing Simulations. *Operations Res*. 22, 72-78.

[10] HEIDELBERGER, P. (1977). Variance Reduction Techniques for Simulations of Markov Processes. Technical Report, Department of Operations Research, Stanford University.

[11] HILLIER, F. S. and LIEBERMAN, G. J. (1974). Introduction to Operations Research. 2nd Ed. Holden-Day, San Francisco.

[12] HORDIJK, A., IGLEHART, D. L., and SCHASSBERGER, R. (1976). Discrete Time Methods for Simulating Continuous Time Markov Chains. Advances Appl. Prob. 8, 772-788.

[13] IGLEHART, D. L. (1975). Simulating Stable Stochastic Systems, V: Comparison of Ratio Estimators. Naval Res. Logist. Quart. 22, 554-565.

[14] IGLEHART, D. L. (1975). Simulating Stable Stochastic Systems, VII: Selecting the Best System. Technical Report No. 86-17, Control Analysis Corporation, Palo Alto, California. To appear in Management Sci. 23 (1977).

[15] IGLEHART, D. L. (1975). Statistical Analysis of Simulations. Technical Report No. 86-18, Control Analysis Corporation, Palo Alto, California.

[16] IGLEHART, D. L. (1975). The Regenerative Method for Simulation Analysis, Technical Report No. 86-20, Control Analysis Corporation, Palo Alto, California. To appear in Current Trends in Programming Methodology, Volume 3, Software Modeling and Its Impact on Performance, Edited by K. M. Chandy and R. T. Yeh. Prentice-Hall, Englewood Cliffs, N. J.

[17] IGLEHART, D. L. (1976). Simulating Stable Stochastic Systems, VI: Quantile Estimation. J. Assoc. Comput Mach. 23, 347-360.

[18] IGLEHART, D. L. (1977). Regenerative Simulations. (Forthcoming).

[19] IGLEHART, D. L. and LEWIS, P. A. W. (1976). Variance Reduction for Regenerative Simulations, I: Internal Control and Stratified Sampling for Queues. Technical Report No. 86-22, Control Analysis Corporation, Palo Alto, California.

[20] KABAK, I. W. (1968). Stopping Rules for Queueing Simulations. Operations Res. 16, 431-437.

[21] LAVENBERG, S.S., MOELLER, T. L. and SAUER, C. H. (1977). Concomitant Control Variables Applied to the Regenerative Simulation of Queueing Systems. Research Report RC 6413, IBM Thomas J. Watson Research Center, Yorktown Heights, New York.

[22] LAVENBERG, S. S. and SAUER, C. H. (1977). Sequential Stopping Rules for the Regenerative Method of Simulation. Research Report RC 6412, IBM Thomas J. Watson Research Center, Yorktown Heights, New York.

[23] LEMOINE, A., MITRA, A. and NEWRUCK, F. (1975). On the Simulation of Some Stable Stochastic Systems. Technical Report No. 199, Department of Mathematical Sciences, Clemson University.

[24] ROBINSON, D. W. (1976). Determination of Run Length in Simulations of Stable Stochastic Systems. Technical Report No. 86-21, Control Analysis Corporation, Palo Alto, California.

[25] SEILA, A. F. (1976). Quantile Estimation Methods in Discrete Event Simulations of Stochastic Systems. Technical Report No. 76-12, Curriculum in Operations Research and Systems Analysis, University of North Carolina, Chapel Hill.

Lecture Notes in Economics and Mathematical Systems

For information about Vols. 1–95 please contact your bookseller or Springer-Verlag